Wayne McKinnon's
Complete Guide to E-mail

Grant

E-mail Rules!

Wayne McKinnon

Wayne McKinnon's
Complete Guide to E-mail

How to effectively use and not be abused by E-mail

by Wayne R. McKinnon

Ryshell Books
Nepean, Ontario
1-888-712-6224

First Edition, Second Printing 1999

Wayne McKinnon's Complete Guide to E-mail

Send E-mail to info@ITcoach.com *to request reprint permission, or contact Ryshell Books Suite 531, 900 Greenbank Road, Nepean, Ontario Canada K2J 4C5 Telephone: 1-888-712-6224*

Cataloguing in Publication Data

McKinnon, Wayne R., 1963-
Wayne McKinnon's Complete Guide to E-mail

Includes bibliographical references and index.
ISBN 0-9683203-0-9

1. Electronic Mail Systems. I. Title. II. Title: Complete Guide to E-mail

TK5105.73.M37 1999 004.692 C99-002267-6

Cover Design by Patti Herson
Publication Design, Layout and Graphics by Heather Murdoch
Edited and Indexed by Elizabeth Macfie

Printed in Canada
10 9 8 7 6 5 4 3 2 1

Other books by Wayne McKinnon

"NetWare to Windows NT Complete:
Integration and Migration"
(McGraw-Hill)

How to Contact the Author

Wayne McKinnon provides consulting services to business and associations internationally. For information about these services as well as inquiries about his availability for speeches and seminars please contact Wayne directly.

Wayne McKinnon,
The Information Technology Coach™

E-mail: Info@ITcoach.com

Fax: (613) 825-4895

Phone: (613) 762-4608

Internet: http://www.ITcoach.com

Acknowledgments

A funny thing happened when I sat down to write this book. Once the title was established I was bombarded with E-mail, voice-mail and faxes providing suggestions for the book. Could it be that everyone wanted to be included in the acknowledgment... or rather that this topic strikes a chord with so many people they just can't contain themselves!

I would like to thank:

Jamie Miller for his contribution to E-mail security and information warfare;

Arnold Villeneuve for incessantly pointing out compatibility problems with our many communication methods we use;

Randy Evans for providing more technical knowledge than I could possibly include in these pages;

The many participants who have attended my courses and workshops for their book title and content suggestions;

Dr. Lynda Falkenstein for pushing me in the right direction when I got lost, and Dr. Julie Miller for her contribution;

David Songco for making sure that this book-writing roller coaster had more highs than lows by providing continuous encouragement—in his words: *"This is fantastic, you gotta get this out there!"*

Dave Kemp for generously sharing his time.

Bob Urichuck and Denis Cauvier for leading by example.

John Platts for planting the seeds for this book and providing valuable feedback along the way;

Tom Kingsbury, Carlos Dwarka, Scott Weingust and Craig Senior for their input and support;

Elizabeth Macfie and Heather Murdoch for their hard work completing the editing and layout and Patti Herson for designing the book cover.

My many clients who have invited me to solve their complex technology and people problems;

But most of all, Heather, my wife, who has an incredible ability to see what is right.

I dedicate this book to Shelby Elizabeth and Ryan James.

Here's what people are saying about...

Wayne McKinnon's Complete Guide to E-mail:

"E-mail can save you time or waste your time. In just a few minutes this book shows you how to get the best from your E-mail while avoiding the traps."

Dave C. Songco
Assistant Director for Engineering and Programs,
DCRT, National Institutés of Health

"Embracing new technology can be difficult. This book contains the basic principles and proven disciplines for mastering your electronic communications."

Bob Urichuck
Author of
The 12 Disciplines to Living the Life of Your Dreams: Master Self-motivation and Personal Leadership
Founding President, Canadian Association of Professional Speakers - Ottawa Chapter

"The use of E-mail is rapidly becoming a necessity in all lines of business. Too often the E-mail vehicle is misused due to inexperience on the part of the sender.

This book clearly identifies the many common pitfalls that are there waiting to clog up one's day, and offers practical as well as common-sense solutions to avoid those pitfalls.

Wayne offers a clear and easy-to-understand description of working with E-mail, that doesn't require the reader to have a degree in computer science!"

David Booker,
President,
Learning Tree Canada

Contents

Foreword
by Anna Lee Chabot

Choices, choices, choices! E-mail, fax or snail-mail? Remember when snail-mail was the communication vehicle of choice? Then facsimile transmission took over, and now it's electronic mail—and I haven't even mentioned the telephone!

The written word is still the preferred medium of business communication. What *has* changed is the number of transmission choices we now have: how do we want to send a given message, and how soon does it need to arrive?

To convey almost any message accurately and with any degree of permanence, and for the legal benefits, the written word is here to stay.

Concurrent with the revolution in communications technology, the world around us has speeded up and shrunk. The need to communicate clearly, rapidly and frequently has increased—often with people we have never met in countries we have never visited.

Which came first, technology or globalism? The question is a chicken-and-egg riddle that this book does not attempt to solve.

What this book does provide is clear, logically ordered, jargon-free guidance to help you to use E-mail in the most effective manner for your particular needs, in the office, at home or on the road.

When Wayne McKinnon asked me to write this foreword, I began by imagining the ideal guide to using E-mail to its best advantage. After I had read Wayne's work, I realized how much I had learned and what an easy read it had been. Even entertaining!

Can you think of any user's manual that you would actually call entertaining? But then, this is no typical user's manual. Wayne teaches the fundamentals of E-mail communication to help you develop successful habits.

Wayne also shares with us his passion for solving the communication problems that arise from this electronic medium.

As a consultant, Wayne has designed electronic communication systems and he knows the pain of the novice and experienced user alike. He has been there himself! In this guide, Wayne helps us adapt our practices and our thinking. He shows us how to take advantage of the benefits of a business communication medium that is here to stay and will be a key tool in the next millennium.

As with most business people today, time is one of my most precious commodities. I receive more and more messages every day. Indeed, sometimes after being away from the office for just a few hours, I am almost overwhelmed by the number of messages that await me on my return. This book has taught me how to deal with the overload and has actually bought me more time.

As President of Meeting Professionals International, a global meeting-industry association, I know how important excellent communication habits and skills are for one's professional image. In an international business environment, the timeliness and quality of our communications count. They reflect directly on us the senders, and on our organizations.

When I travel, I like to know that I can stay in touch with the important people and activities in my life—in my job, my volunteer position and my family. In the chapter "Tips for the Traveler," Wayne helps us to first anticipate the challenges we may encounter and then to equip ourselves in advance to overcome them.

Wayne's style and approach make this book an easy read. You can quickly find the solution to a particular problem by scanning the concise headings throughout each chapter. You can pick up the book for five minutes at a time and benefit. Alternately, read through from front to back for a comprehensive, practical course in communicating electronically.

I know you will find *Wayne McKinnon's Complete Guide to E-mail* extremely valuable, as I have. E-mail is a communications choice that is here to stay. With this book as your guide, you will gain mastery of this increasingly important tool.

Anna Lee Chabot, CMP
Head, Meetings and Assemblies
The Royal College of Physicians and Surgeons of Canada
and President 1997-1998
Meeting Professionals International

Introduction:

Make the Most of E-mail's Power

How often do you meet someone who asks for your E-mail address or perhaps offers you theirs? Have you overheard someone talking about how many E-mail messages they have, or how they just have to check their E-mail? Do you wonder whether this technology is the right tool for your workplace if you're not already connected? Or perhaps you use E-mail and are wondering how you can do so more effectively. Can E-mail be used as a marketing channel to distribute information quickly and cheaply? How does E-mailing compare to your existing methods of communication?

Or perhaps your concern is the policies that your organization should put in place to cover the legal aspects of using E-mail.

I cover all those topics in this book. I also deal with tools and techniques that will allow you to work more efficiently, including how to cut down on the amount of time you spend checking E-mail and responding to requests for information.

On a recent business trip, I overheard three conversations—in an elevator, a hotel lobby and at an airport: people complaining that, when they checked their E-mail that morning, it didn't work. That was in two cities in less than two hours. How often does your E-mail connection break down, and what can you do to avoid it?

In the elevator to my hotel room on another trip, I heard a person discussing the problems she was having with E-mail. "I have a gazillion E-mails and it feels weird not plugging in 15 times a day. I'm going crazy!" She was describing her feelings of isolation caused by not having a method of checking E-mail. And when travelers *do* connect, they are often inundated with messages and wish they had an effective way to deal with the workload.

Then there are those people who feel that the amount of E-mail messages they receive in a day defines how important they are. Watching for new E-mail messages can be addictive. Fortunately, there are ways to handle the compulsion to repeatedly press "Check for Messages."

If you have never used E-mail and want to but are intimidated, realize that E-mail is one of the simplest tools you can use on your personal computer. You don't need to be technically-minded at all. If you have ever left voice mail, you will probably catch on to E-mail very quickly. And you can learn a few simple rules to make the communication process efficient.

Perhaps you are connected to E-mail and are swamped with the amount of information you receive every day. You need to find ways to prioritize the information you receive and to automate some of the process. In this book I tell you about tools that will make your job simpler.

I offer you a basic explanation of how the technology works, what it can do for you, and what tools can help you accomplish your goals. When you press "Send," where does your message go? How does it get from your work station to the destination computer? What can happen to it along the way? The more you understand about the process, the more likely your message and its attachments are to arrive complete and secure.

If you are a technical person, please realize that the average businessperson is focusing on their job, and the technology is just one more tool they use to be effective and save time. And you non-technical readers, please understand that many of the technical people around you are willing to help but their tolerance might be just a little low because of the volume of technical problems they have to solve daily.

I encourage both technical and non-technical parties to spend time trying to understand the other side's point of view. Instead of fixing the small problems with Band-Aids, take a step back and ask, "What is our common problem and how can we solve it using the tools that we have?" We need to make an effort to understand E-mail so that we can use the technology as effectively as possible.

The Seven Sections of This Book

- The first describes problems you may very well encounter, and the best practices to use in those cases.
- The second coaches you on communication skills to make sure your message is understood.
- Part Three is about how to avoid the addiction and burnout that can be caused by getting more information than you can possibly deal with.
- Part Four shows you how to use E-mail in your marketing campaign. One of the biggest issues on the Internet today is spamming—the mass-broadcasting of E-mail messages. I advise you on how to make contacts and distribute marketing information without sending out mass mailings and thus being branded a spammer.
- Part Five is a behind-the-scenes look at the technology that transports E-mail messages.
- Part Six is for travelers: on the road, in hotel rooms, or working from remote offices. You can use these tips on the days that you work from home, too. We will look at tools and strategies for sending and checking your messages, without high communication costs.
- And Part Seven is about E-mail policies: why companies need them and what users should know about their company's policies.

I am confident that you will enjoy this book. It will answer a great many of your questions and make you much more effective using this marvelous technology.

And let's keep in touch. If you have ideas for future editions or would like more information visit my Web site (http://www.ltcoach.com) for tips, news, and technology updates.

Part I

Take the E-mail Challenge

Chapter 1-1

The E-mail Explosion

"Messaging is my most important application."

"When I look at how much time I spend working with spreadsheets and word processors versus E-mail, I find that I spend over five times as much time in E-mail as anything else. It's perhaps the most mission- critical application for Microsoft in terms of running the company."

Bill Gates, Chairman and CEO,
Microsoft Corporation

Today, E-mail has become a way of life for many corporate computer users. The Internet has also become an extension of many of our corporate networks that allow us to communicate not only with the people around us but with people in other companies.

On September 23, 1996, a survey by the San Francisco-based Odyssey Market Research firm found that, for the first time, E-mail surpassed research, news and other information as the number-one activity for consumers who go on-line on the Internet at home. And according to the survey, 32 percent of respondents said E-mail was the main reason for going on-line, followed by 25 percent for research, 22 percent for news and information and 19 percent for entertainment. In a similar survey in January of that year only 21 percent of respondents had signed up principally for E-mail while 21 percent used the Net mostly for research, 24 percent for news and information and 18 percent for entertainment.

The one thing that is clear from this is that E-mail has become the driving force behind connectivity globally on the Internet as well as within our organizations. Many of the organizations that I deal with set up their own cross country corporate networks, primarily to transmit their E-mail.

Once E-mail is in place as a driving force behind the corporate network, other applications begin to take advantage of the infrastructure. In some organizations, E-mail has become so popular that managers are trying to find ways to reduce the flow of messages in order to prevent E-mail from overwhelming the communication lines.

Bill Gates once said that in order for the Internet to become truly successful it needed what he referred to as a killer app, an application that you just have to have. Today, if you look at the primary use of both public and corporate networks, E-mail rules!

E-mail started off as a convenient way to send brief messages and was not then taken as seriously as it is now. Today, millions of people from Fortune 500 businesses to small enterprises to individuals use E-mail daily in place of telephone calls, faxes, courier shipments and letter mail. By giving individuals the ability to communicate around the world efficiently, inexpensively and quickly, E-mail has become the communication tool of choice. As in the case of Bill Gates and Microsoft, most corporations can't function without E-mail today. It has become the primary method of communication for projects and planning, decisions and delegating.

Not everyone has E-mail

If you are an E-mail user, you probably have become so comfortable with this technology that you assume almost everyone has E-mail. We shouldn't forget that there are a tremendous number of people in companies and market sectors who aren't connected, or perhaps have just started to use E-mail and aren't yet as effective as you.

With the advancements in computer telephony (telephone technology) integration, soon all of your communication methods will be interconnected. A message sent to a list of recipients can be automatically sent via each recipient's preferred communication method, be it fax, telephone or E-mail.

E-mail is visual voice mail

Within many organizations, E-mail quickly became an effective communication tool as people adopted the technology and learned that it could replace other means of communication. Compared to voice mail, E-mail messages can be listed, sorted and even previewed. The recipient can get an idea of the topic and importance of each message without having to read each one.

Many people are visual learners. They understand better by seeing things on paper than by trying to put together a mental picture as they listen to your message. Furthermore, using voice mail, the sender often makes up the message as they go along. Using E-mail, it is easier to compose your thoughts and make sure you cover what is necessary. E-mail allows the recipient to quickly identify the important points in a well-composed message.

By including your E-mail address on your business card you allow people to communicate with you using the medium of their choice.

Today, E-mail addresses on business cards are just as common as fax numbers and telephone numbers. In fact it wasn't that long ago that fax numbers were a novelty on business cards. I was amazed to find that my relatives in southern Manitoba, a hundred miles from anywhere, have E-mail. It struck me that if farmers in southern Manitoba have E-mail to talk to people around the world then isn't it about time that all business people plug in?

E-mail speeds up communication

You might argue that E-mail is a slower method of communication than a long distance telephone call, but it doesn't need to be. Often, the hours that we spend on the telephone are not as productive as we would like them to be. They are not as structured. When you send an E-mail message you can think your thoughts through clearly, you can refine them, you can send off the message, you can get the response that you want back. If long distance telephone costs are an issue, you can use E-mail to carry on a daily dialogue rather than make long distance calls once every few months.

One of the advantages of E-mail is that it is not dependent on other people's schedules. We don't have to call at a certain time when we know that they will be there. An E-mail message can be sent at any time of day or night. The recipient can respond at their convenience.

I find E-mail extremely convenient if I have a question or a thought that I need to share late at night. Rather than wait until the next day to make a telephone call I can type an E-mail message and send it off on the spot.

E-mail is cheaper than a speeding courier

You can send rich attachments with most E-mail systems. You can send documents, spreadsheets and presentations for review. Maybe you want to include some photographs. The technology is not perfect yet, though. The format of the document must be compatible with the recipient's software. Additionally, files must be converted into attachments using one of many electronic standards. Your recipient's E-mail system must support this standard, or your attachment will be worthless junk.

Also, be aware of the cost that you or your organization is paying for messages. With some systems you may be charged based on the volume or size of information you send. Consider compression software to shrink the attachment before sending it. This will both save time and space.

E-mail is unintrusive

Unlike in the case of telephone calls, recipients control E-mail communication. They can schedule when they will check, read and respond to their E-mail, yet their door is always open. People will send an E-mail to someone who otherwise might seem unapproachable.

A ringing telephone, or someone at your office door, is an interruption. The more interruptions during the day, the less effective you will be. Once interrupted, it can take you up to fifteen minutes to get back into a flow. Another interruption, and you'll spend another fifteen minutes getting back to where you were.

E-mail, being unintrusive, is more effective than either a trip to visit somebody or a telephone call.

Don't give up on the telephone entirely, though. A telephone call is much more personal, and by answering your phone yourself you give the impression of being accessible to a broader range of people and having an open-door policy. Plus you have not restricted your communication to one medium.

E-mail messages are great reminders

A verbal message is one more thing for you to keep track of, and you might forget it. I pass someone in a hallway at work and they say, "Please send me the latest document that you worked on. I would like a copy of it." Or, "Do you remember the name of that restaurant that we went to? I would like to entertain a client there." Or, "My computer is broken. Can you make sure that you get someone out to fix it?" I have good intentions, but a weak memory.

Ask people to send you an E-mail message as a reminder. You will automatically receive their E-mail address, and any details that you might want to add to a problem-tracking system or electronic calendar and phone book / contact manager. Many E-mail systems let you categorize your incoming messages and store them. An E-mail reminder can be friendly and effective.

E-mail shouldn't entirely replace face-to-face conversations

Over the years, we've had many different methods of communicating with one another. Face-to-face meetings are still popular because body language plays a pretty important role in delivering our message. Don't use E-mail as an easy way out when a phone call or meeting really is necessary—particularly in a dispute. We will deal with this topic further in Chapter 1-2.

Use E-mail to create a virtual corporation

E-mail has allowed us to expand the walls of our corporations so we can easily deal with people around the world. People meet new contacts electronically, on the Internet and other on-line services such as America Online (AOL) and CompuServe. Like pen pals, distance workers can become close friends and allies without ever meeting.

There are many message service providers that can set up E-mail-based virtual corporations or virtual post offices for traveling workers who have no home base. For example, one company that I work with does not have an internal E-mail system at their head office, because only a small administrative staff is based there. The sales force is always on the road. Everyone, including the administrative staff, is connected to a service provider who maintains their mail system. Therefore, they don't pay the overhead costs of operating an internal E-mail system, yet they have access to a system they can all connect to. And such private networks are secure, unlike the Internet, which can be made secure but is not necessarily so. Consequently, messages on private networks are never seen by unauthorized eyes.

Send to multiple recipients easily

One of the advantages of an E-mail system is that it is simple, easy and cost effective to send one message to more than one recipient at the same time. Picking up the phone to call each individual is time-consuming, and it also interrupts their day. An E-mail message is like a letter: you can send to many people at the same time. But the cost of distributing a document through the postal service can be high. In Canada a letter costs 48¢, that's $48.00 for 100 letters!

For your E-mail message, you can process a mailing list the way you do a mail merge in your word-processed document to create envelopes for those 100 people. (But be sure to read the section of this book on Marketing with E-mail before you indiscriminately send junk mail.)

The real advantage of E-mail is that the distribution of messages is electronic. There are no paper or printing expenses. The cost of sending depends on the E-mail system you use, but in many cases the cost of sending an E-mail message is much less than using the postal service. Also, the delivery of that electronic message is almost instantaneous—within minutes or hours versus days or weeks.

E-mail is not prejudiced.

If you received an E-mail message from Pat Smith, would you know anything about this person's race, color, religious beliefs, possible disabilities, or even their gender? Pat would have a very good chance of establishing a business relationship with you, avoiding any petty discriminatory feelings you might have based on first-sight impressions.

I wish we lived in a society where personal details never created a barrier to effective communication. But that does happen sometimes, and E-mail can allow someone who might otherwise may be treated unfairly to be on equal footing with everyone else. The only personal detail that E-mail reveals about its sender is that person's name, but that too can be hidden by using an alias.

What is the future of communications?

E-mail is being used more and more in place of other methods of communication. It is replacing face-to-face meetings when there is just a brief matter to discuss. It is replacing fax for sending informal or urgent messages. You might choose E-mail as an alternative to placing a telephone call when the other person is not available, or when you want more time to compose and review your thoughts—not easy to do in a direct conversation. And you can E-mail at any time of the day or night. You can write in your spare time. On the road, you can compose messages while off-line using a laptop or palm-top computer, then send them when you get access to a telephone or other communication link.

E-mail is a step toward the paperless office, replacing some of the work of the fax machine, which requires paper-in and paper-out. Up-to-date electronic fax solutions hook directly into computers, but many people have stayed with the paper fax machine because they are more comfortable with that technology. E-mail systems now allow us to send to both fax and E-mail recipients at the same time, paper-free (yet many people print out their E-mail messages).

When a tool becomes so commonplace that it is accepted as the standard, then that freezes the advancement of technology. Manufacturers sometimes manage to dislodge the old standard with new leading-edge technology, and in some cases that solution evolves into the new standard. Today E-mail rules! Manufacturers will find ways to permeate our world with E-mail. Has your car sent an E-mail message to the dealer alerting them that your vehicle will soon require service yet?

Stay tuned for all-in-one messaging systems that will allow people to contact you using their favorite method: fax, voice, E-mail, or video. You will retrieve these messages using one single tool to read voice messages or listen to E-mail. Much of the technology exists today, and one day soon it will be commonplace.

Chapter 1-2

Preventing People-Problems

"If it wasn't for users my network would be just fine."

-The cry of the over-employed LAN (local area network) administrator

Many of the problems we encounter when using E-mail systems are not directly the fault of any individual user or even individual technology, but are simply oversights. Many people do not understanding why or how E-mailing differs from other forms of communication.

Junk mail can overwhelm the recipient. Before sending any correspondence, be sure the recipient is interested in its content

The most common complaint of E-mail users is "too many messages," and many of the messages are junk mail. That is anything that contains little or no value to the reader and is a nuisance. Those small interruptions steal your attention and break the flow of your day, and can mask important issues.

The term "spam" is used to describe mass mailings or any broadcasted junk mail, and sales information is the worst. Are you a spammer on your corporate network? Are people tired of hearing about your recruitment drive for the company softball team? If you canvass for a worthy cause, post the message by the elevator or visit people at their desks. If you meet with someone in person, you can appeal to his or her emotional side and thus have a higher success rate. If there is any doubt that something that you are about to send may be viewed as junk mail, don't send it! Read Part 4 of this book on using E-mail as a marketing tool, too.

Sending jokes can brighten someone's day, but be sure each recipient considers this practice as valuable as you do

Jokes are junk mail to some people. There is nothing more annoying than being on someone's joke mailing list when you don't want to be.

If you are on a joke list and want off, send a polite response asking to be removed from the list. If you are the sender, pre-qualify the recipients by saying: "I send out jokes from time to time. Would you like to be on my list?" That gives them the opportunity to say no up front rather than having to say later, "Stop doing this, please, you're annoying me."

Beware of off-color jokes. Even if sender and recipient consent, don't forget that your message can be forwarded with your name still attached. Managers have become concerned because if the wrong person sees a message, a harassment charge could be laid against the organization. And racial jokes are not okay. Pick a new topic.

Think twice before forwarding raw data to others

I see it over and over. A real keener on a particular topic collects all sorts of information and passes it on to everyone who may be remotely interested. Most people are not as interested as you think and would much rather ask for specific information when they need it rather than become content experts themselves.

Most junk mail senders mean well. They forward you information that you are not interested in, not realizing the intrusion and confusion they cause. Make E-mailers in your organization aware of the risk of overwhelming others, in order to solve this problem.

Instead, try posting information where all can access it if they want to, rather than storing it themselves. For example, if you would like to access to my resource page, visit http://www.ITcoach.com and select "Resources."

Don't send multiple copies of the same message using multiple communication methods

Too many people will send an E-mail, then send a fax and make a telephone call with the same information. When it is sufficient to leave a voice mail message, following up by E-mail with the same content is redundant. There may be times when it is necessary to cover all of the bases, but not often.

For example, I might call to remind you that there is an E-mail waiting for you with information on the project that we discussed. That is efficient. But going through all of the details again is not necessary.

Use the most suitable method of communication

Recently, a client at a company I was dealing with asked for my help. I sent him an E-mail message and a week later I received a reply along with his fax number and some other requests. He wrote that he would prefer that I fax my response. When I met with him he explained that his organization uses E-mail to send product updates and sales figures to sales staff on the road. E-mail isn't a general communication tool in his company. As a result, he and his staff check their E-mail only once a week. I, on the other hand, use E-mail constantly, and check my electronic in-box once an hour. Be sure to ask what communication method people prefer. Many people are permanently connected to their computer network and receive E-mail messages as they arrive. Those in other organizations, or in a home office, check their E-mail less frequently. Realize that your recipients may use their E-mail systems differently than you do.

If you use E-mail as a method of delegating tasks, do you assume that the recipient will carry out the task without the opportunity to discuss it? If something is truly urgent, a telephone call may be a better way of relaying the importance of the task and discussing alternatives.

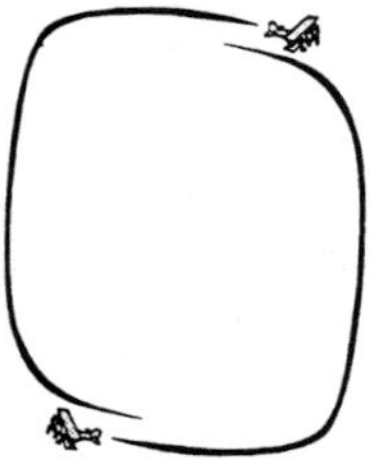

Keep everyone in the loop

When you communicate with a group of people on a project, watch that you don't leave anyone out of loop at any time.

For example, a sales rep with whom I was working was in the process of selling services to a client. The rep sent me an E-mail saying: "Could you please contact my client? I'd like you to discuss technical matters X, Y and Z. Please get back to me and let me know the result."

E-mail was the client's preferred means of communication, and I sent him a message, with a copy to the sales rep to make sure everyone was kept in the loop. The client responded to me, answering my questions about the technical matter.

Next, the sales rep met with the client face-to-face and, based on the technical information I had provided, they agreed on terms. The sales rep E-mailed me that the client intended to go ahead with the project but wanted me to send him a final outline of the tasks that we were going to perform. I E-mailed that list of tasks to the client and I copied the sales rep once again.

The client responded to me by E-mail, "O.K. looks good," so I began work on the project. Then the sales rep called me a few days later: "Wayne, what's going on? Has the client replied? Is he waiting for anything from you? What stage are we at?" I was shocked; I had made the fatal assumption that the sales rep was staying in touch with the client and that when the client said, "O.K., looks good," that the project was a go and the client had notified the sales rep as well. Unbeknownst to me, they had yet to wrap up the terms of the contract and the payment scheme. Our information loop had fallen apart.

Avoid blind copies

A lot of E-mail systems can send blind copies as well as carbon copies. Blind copies let you send a copy to a second recipient without the knowledge of the first recipient. You might send a blind copy to keep someone in the conversation, even if they are not an ongoing member of the information loop. The recipient of your original message can see who you sent carbon copies to; they don't know who received blind copies.

I recommend that you not send blind copies. A person who receives a blind copy may not realize that it was blind and might respond, not knowing you meant to keep their participation a secret. Save your message before sending it, and then send it twice: once to your information loop members, and then to the person you wish to copy without the others' knowledge.

Also be aware that some E-mail gateways may block messages that are sent to the recipient using the BCC (blind copy) field.

How do you know if you have been blind-copied?

Look at the list of recipients. In the example below I sent a message to "nobody@home." I also sent a blind copy to "You the reader". Notice that your name does not appear in the list of recipients in either "To" or "Cc" lines. My name appears as the sender of the message on the "From" line. The only clue that you have been blind copied is that your name does not appear in the list, yet you received the message.

Composing a message and sending a blind copy.

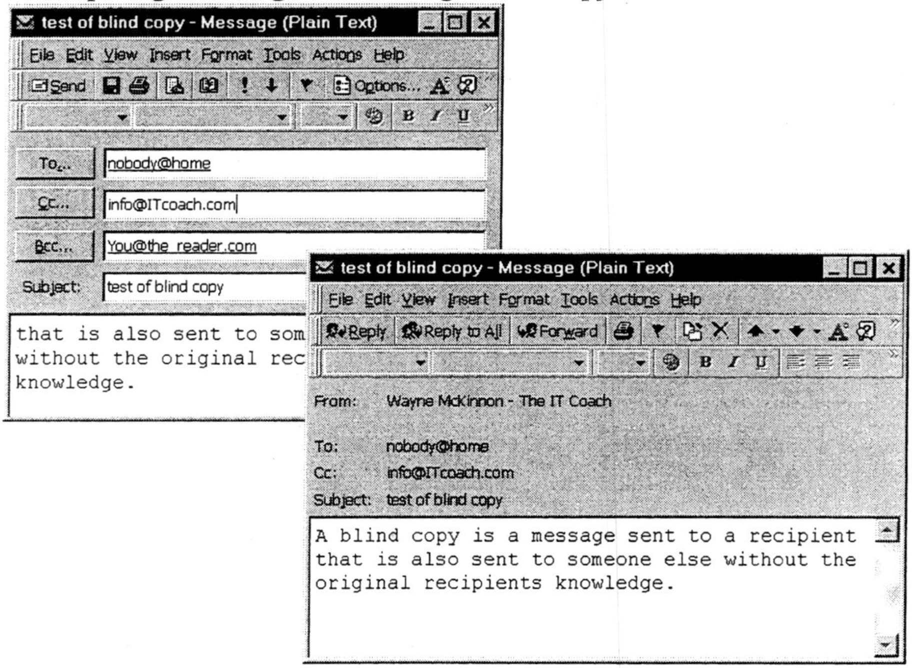

Blind copy received by, "You the reader."

None of the recipients will see your name in the list of recipients.

Don't cry wolf!

In many organizations people are overwhelmed by the amount of messages they receive. If they receive more E-mail than they can possibly handle in a single day, they will begin to ignore messages.

If there is some critical information that you need to pass on to somebody, pick up the telephone or drop by their desk.

Since there is no guarantee that others will read time-sensitive information on time, consider alternate methods. A fax tends to reach the recipient's desk right away. Pick up the telephone or walk across the hall and talk to people if the matter is urgent. Your message is likely not the only one in their Electronic in-box.

To avoid missed messages, investigate some form of E-mail notification. Is your E-mail system able to page you when new messages arrive?

Meanings can be misconstrued

As with any form of communication, the meaning of an E-mail is open to interpretation. You may have meant sarcasm but the recipient thought you were serious. You could end up with strained relationships as a result. To discuss sensitive matters when a careful interpersonal touch is important, a telephone or face-to-face discussion is most effective.

Here is an example of a message that was misunderstood because of lack of explanatory detail: a company sent a message saying that this year they have a deficit of $100,000. The recipient took that to mean losses in addition to the already-forecasted deficit / bad news. But in fact the message attempted to communicate the good news that while the predicted deficit was actually closer to $1,000,000, the company got it down to $100,000 for this quarter. Think carefully about how the reader might understand your words.

When you reply to a message, say more than just "O.K., I agree." State what you're agreeing to or what the next step that you expect is. For example, instead of just replying "O.K.," say, "O.K., can you send me a proposal of the cost of this service, please?" Don't assume that the recipients know what you mean. Spell out what everyone is agreeing to and restate the terms.

Delivery is not guaranteed

Unfortunately, E-mail is not like Fedex. Yes, many systems provide delivery notification, and your company's system might provide an audit trail, but across the global Internet E-mail correspondence is treated on a "best attempt to deliver" basis. There is no guarantee that your message will arrive. E-mail is forwarded along the network from one location to another, until it eventually gets where it is going. If you need guaranteed secure service you need a private network.

Don't assume that your message was read

Maybe your message was delivered but there is no guarantee that it was actually read or understood by the recipient. An effective follow-up is always worthwhile.

Thank you

Too much politeness results in long and excess messages

Thank you

Thank you!

You may be overwhelming others with the number of communications that you send. If you receive a series of messages from one person try sending just one acknowledgment for all the messages. Establish with your communication partners what types of messages require acknowledgment.

Should you combine many topics in one message?

While this might seem efficient, it complicates tasks involving several people. The whole team may not need to see all of the items, so break them down into separate messages for the appropriate people. This way, recipients can respond more easily, and can forward selected items to others.

Everyone won't remember the previous conversation

I can't tell you how many times I have received a message thanking me, or asking for more information, and I can't remember what my original message said. Some E-mail programs automatically copy the message you are responding to into your reply. If yours doesn't, be specific in your message or cut and paste parts of the message you are replying to into your response. It is standard to insert > before any such reference text.

Example:

```
>I will be in your area next week.
>If you want to save on travel costs
>I could speak to your group then.

Thanks, Wayne. We could schedule you for
Tuesday morning. How about meeting for
dinner when you arrive Monday night;
say, 5:00 at The Place Next Door?
```

Write a descriptive subject line

The subject line of your message allows the recipient to easily decide if your message is worth reading. It also helps in finding important information in a overfilled in-box. Write a meaningful subject line. If you reply to a message and the topic changes, change the subject line to reflect the new topic.

When a brief response is required sometimes the subject line alone suffices. To make the message even briefer you can include your telephone number in your address.

Example:

```
From: The ITcoach (613) 762-4608
SUBJECT: AGREED; SEE YOU AT 5:00pm
```

WARNING: Some E-mail applications do not display the entire contents of a lengthy subject line, so you may want to copy the subject line and paste it in the body of the message.

Consider writing a summary of the message in the first few lines of text, since many E-mail programs provide a preview feature that displays the first few lines of each message.

Consider the recipient's connection before sending large attachments

Speed is an issue, as is the cost of connection. You cause undue stress on your corporate network if you send large attachments that could be distributed in other ways. This is particularly true if you send the attachment to multiple recipients, because many E-mail systems send and store a separate copy for every person on your distribution list.

Some E-mail systems use efficient store-once technology, meaning that the message gets stored once and only a pointer to the attachment is placed in the recipients' in-boxes.

For a traveler, long-distance costs can be expensive. To limit costs and usage, some companies restrict the size of incoming messages. In any case, large attachments take up excess storage space. It might be more effective to send everyone a notice that they can find the information in a central location if they are interested.

Avoid writing long-winded messages

If your messages are clear, concise and to the point—voice mail, telephone calls, or memos—they have a much higher chance of being read, interpreted correctly, and responded to.

Example:

```
To:      you, the reader
From:    Wayne, the ITcoach
Subject: Long-winded messages

Be clear and concise in your message.
Provide the answers to these questions:

• who
• what
• when
• where
• why

Continue with more detail for the
recipient to read at his or her
discretion.

Make sure your message includes the
points that you know are important to
the recipient and summarize them at the
top of the message.
```

Messages are often written in haste

Since E-mail is quick and easy to compose, you will be tempted to write notes and send them immediately to get them out of the way. But remember that your recipients cannot question you about unclear details, as they could in a face-to-face conversation. A handy aspect of E-mail is that you can compose a message, save it, and come back to it later for review. Take advantage of this and think your messages through. Be sure you have answered the questions. Are your points clear or have you left room for misinterpretation?

Notify others when you will be away

People get annoyed when their messages are being ignored. As a courtesy to those who rely on your expertise, notify them when you are away. In Part 6 of this book I will show you how to automatically let message senders know that you are away.

Summary: making the most of the human element of E-mail

- Before sending a message, ask yourself if the recipient would be interested in it, then ask them.
- Become a source of answers, not of raw data.
- If you choose to send jokes, make sure the recipient is willing. Avoid off-color jokes.
- Avoid long-winded messages.
- Summarize points in bullet form at the beginning of the message.
- Use the recipient's preferred communication method; don't send him or her multiple copies of the same message.
- Do not assume everyone uses E-mail the same way or as frequently as you do.
- Pick up the telephone or meet when a personal approach is most appropriate.
- Send attachments in the way that puts the least possible burden on the system.

Chapter 1-3

Avoiding Technology Traps

"On a recent business trip, I overheard three people complain that their E-mail did not work that morning. That's three people in two cities in less than an hour. Could they all be working for the same company?"

Although I called the previous chapter "People Problems," you could argue that all of the problems in that chapter were technological. (Of course, the techies would argue that they are all people problems.) ☺

Still, I find it easiest to separate the challenges that are more user-related from those caused by the hardware and software.

Synchronize directories

The biggest E-mail technology problem that organizations face is directory synchronization. A corporate E-mail system has a central directory, (or address book) listing the E-mail addresses of all staff. If the organization has multiple mail servers or dissimilar E-mail systems tied together, keeping this list current can be extremely difficult. Even using automated updates, things can still go wrong.

If the various departments in your organization have E-mail systems from different manufacturers, the E-mail administrators will have to make a special effort to maintain a master list of company employees in one directory. If anyone is added to one system, the changes must be propagated to other systems. In many cases, this is a manual process, or a batch process that has to be launched every night.

Synchronize your personal address book

With many E-mail systems, there is no way to easily synchronize your personal address book and the organization's master list. If someone moves to another location in your organization, their E-mail account may be re-located to an E-mail server in their new department or branch. As a result, his or her old E-mail address may no longer work.

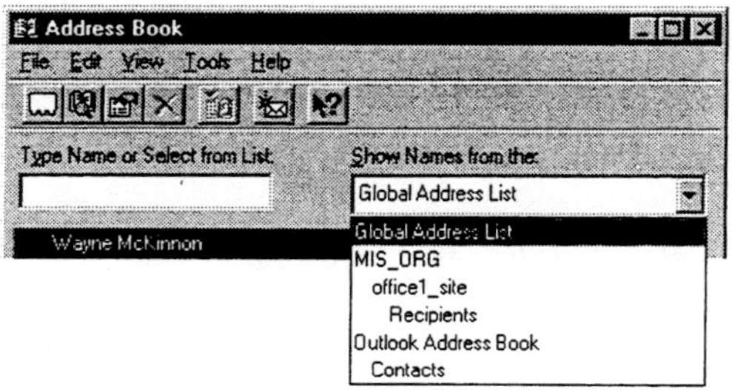

Fig 1-3.1

Try selecting their name from the corporate list and see if that works. While it is convenient to have your own personal list, you may simply find that it is less work to use the corporate directory.

Microsoft Outlook can allow you to choose from a number of address books.

If you are not part of a large organization, you probably maintain your own E-mail address list. You know how difficult it is to keep track of everyone as they move around, but a solution is here. Lightweight Directory Access Protocol (LDAP), a standard that vendors have agreed on, allows E-mail clients to look at corporate directories. It will also provide a way to keep address books on different systems up to date as the standard evolves.

Any of the newer E-mail clients such as versions of Netscape and Outlook dating from 1998 or later are LDAP-compliant. As organizations begin to use LDAP you will be able to query their address lists right off of their Web site.

Connecting can be a problem

Connectivity is usually not a problem in a corporate network, though if you've ever come in on a Monday morning and found the file server down, you know how frustrating this can be. But remote connectivity problems do happen to people who use E-mail while traveling.

One company with worldwide connections through a service provider found that when their staff traveled in India they couldn't connect, due to the low quality of the telephone lines. Although they could make phone calls, the poor signal quality could not support electronic communications.

You should also be aware that not all hotel telephone switch systems can handle computer connections, although most of the better ones do. Read more in Part 6 of this book: "Tips for the Traveler."

E-mail systems are not always compatible

```
If you use Internet mail you may notice =
messages that appear with symbols consisting =
of an equal sign followed by two characters =
as you see here. This indicates incompatibility =
between your E-mail system and that of the sender. =
```

The Internet standard for E-mail systems is Simple Message Transfer Protocol (SMTP). Although most E-mail systems use 8-bit SMTP, the older standard is 7-bit. It is these older systems that cause the problems.

All E-mail clients offer some degree of customization. This example shows how to select your preferences using Netscape Mail.

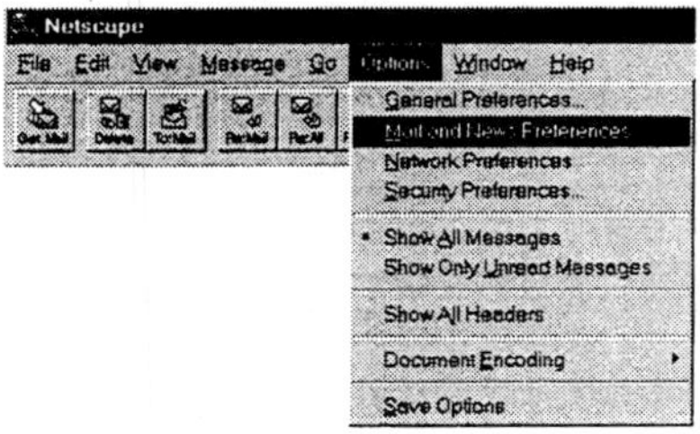

Fig 1-3.2

When you send a message you can configure your system to use the formatting standard preferred by the majority of your recipients.

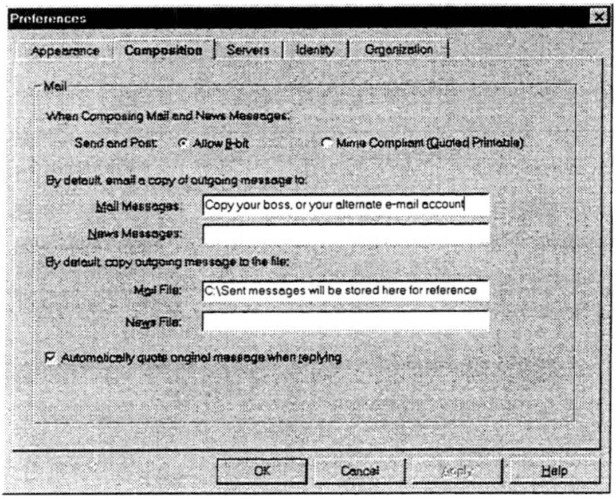

Fig. 1-3.3

Other mixes of characters indicate difficulty handling attachments.

The older standard was UU-encoding that represented pictures and documents as a series of letters that had to be decoded to represent the original attachment.

The latest standard is Multipurpose Internet Mail Extensions (MIME), although you may also encounter other encoding or compression methods, such as BinHex (commonly used for Macintosh computers), TAR (a Unix utility), and ZIP.

To decode these messages:

- Save the message as a text file.
- Convert the attachment using a third-party utility such as WinZip 6.3 that recognizes the encoding format. (Alternatively, a plug-in may be available for your mail program that will allow automatic conversion when you view the document.)

Here is what a BinHex file attachment might look like before decoding:


```
:$(GKFR*PEQ)Q,R4TCJ!r2cmr,5dY,3%!!!9@2J!!!!$+9NP*+J!)!!!!%
J$q!!3!!3!!!!!!!!!!!!3!!3!!!&)#!!!"!3!!3!!!%`#!!!#!33!!!!J!
!!!$!3!!3!!!!%!!!!'!3!!3!!!!%!!!!+!3!!3!!!!%!!!!4!33!!3!!!
1B"!!!5!3!!3!!!!%!!!!9!3!!3!!!!%!!!!@!33!!3!!!%`#!!!A!33!!
3!!!&K8"3!D!38!!3!!!1B!!!!E!38!!3!!!1i!!!!F!3-
!!3!!!!%!!!!S!3-
!!3!!!!)!!!!b!3)!&!!!!2B!!!!l!3)!*J!!!"i"!!!!!!!!PJ!!!!%!!
!#@!!!!!3!!!$%a,6)d,6%j16)!!!!!!!!!!!!!!!!!!!!!!!!!!!!!!!!
!!!!!!!!a16Nb)%&$3e966dC8)%P13b`J38a)&**4dK88b"5490&8PC&4!
!!!!!!!!!!!!!!!!!!!!!!!!!!!!!!!!!!!!!!!!!!!!!!!!!!!!!!!!!!
!!!!!!!!!!!!!!!!!!!!!!!!!!!!!!!!!!!!!!!!!!!!!!!!!!!!!!!!!!
!!!!!!!!!!!!!!!!!!!!!!!!!!!!!!!!!!!!!!!!!!!!!!!!!!!!!!!!!!
!!!!!!!!!!!!!!!!!!!!!!!!!!!!!!!!!!!!!!!!!("cG(*cFR0cFh9dG(
4eGA4dG(0dFh"cFR"`FR9cGA4cFh4bFR9dG(*`Fh0bGA4dG(4cFR*bFh0b
FhCcFh"cFfp[F'p`F'pbFR"bF'p`FR"[EQpcGA"[F'pYFRf(LSk4P*@6MS
&fGRq"JB1$K)1$IA4RBf&MBf4MBejKBf&MB@0MAQ&KBf0NBf4PB@&HBepK
Af0MBf0MBf0MBf4IB9pIB@&MBepHB@&KBf&KB@&NBejIAepKB@&KB@0KB@
0IB@4KBf&KB@&KB@&MBf&NBf0IBejIB@0KB9pIAepMB9pKAf&PB@&MC@&H
B9pIC'0MC'4MC'0MAepIBf0MBf0KB@9MBf9KBf0PBf4KAf&NBf&NBf0MAf
&KB@0MB@&NBf4KAf0KB@0MBf&PBf&NC'4MBf4KBepKBf0MB@0KB9pMBf4N
C@0NBf&MB@0MC'&NB@0MC'4MB@0MBf0KBep
```


See Part 5 of this book for more solutions.

Where did these body parts come from?

Different E-mail systems represent message components differently. When attachments are passed between two dissimilar systems, the attachments can be messed up, particularly if the message has passed through an E-mail system that uses the X.400 standard (as opposed to SMTP). (Don't worry, all you need to know is that the people who create names for standards using numbers do things differently than the ones who prefer letters.) ☺

The result is often that attachments will lose their names and instead will be named bodypart 1, bodypart 2 etc. To make it easier for the recipient to rename these files, provide the proper file names in the message for reference. For example:

```
To: You the Reader

From: Wayne, The ITcoach

Attached are the files you requested. I have
included my Information Technology report for
March and April.

File 1   April.doc

File 2   March.doc
```

Figure 1-3.4

Message Formatting

Regardless of the E-mail system you connect to, messages that are written using one E-mail client may not appear the same on another.

Your E-mail application may automatically format text by using a feature called autowrap. While it may be useful for keeping cars dry during the winter<grin>, autowrap prevents the line of text from extending beyond the screen.

The problem occurs when the message is sent to someone who uses a different E-mail client that does not support the autowrap feature. Designed properly, the E-mail application will begin a new line automatically.

This is rarely a problem in a corporate network where everyone connects to the same E-mail system. But if the messages travel over the Internet or into another mail system, the message may appear as one continuous line of text that extends beyond the screen.

In order to ensure that your message can be read by others, put line breaks or carriage returns at the end of each line of text. A safe limit is 80 characters of text per line. Yes, this is inconvenient, but so is receiving a message that cannot be read easily.

Example: your message may appear as one continuous line of text.

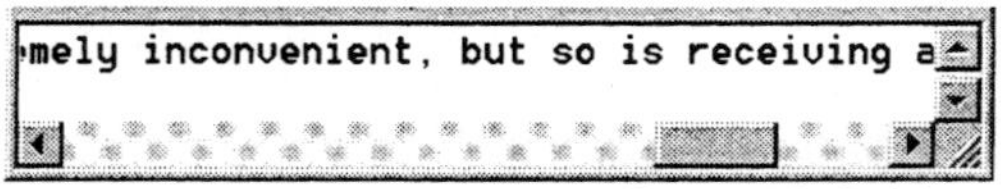

Figure 1-3.4A

Choose applications that are E-mail-enabled

If you use E-mail as your primary method of communication, chose applications that are E-mail-enabled. You will find it quite convenient to work within a document and be able to send a copy to one of your associates for review without having to first save the document, open the mail application, select the document, select the recipient and finally send the attachment.

Before making your purchasing decision, be aware that you might lose application compatibility if you ever change your E-mail program. Many applications that work well with one mail program may have problems with another.

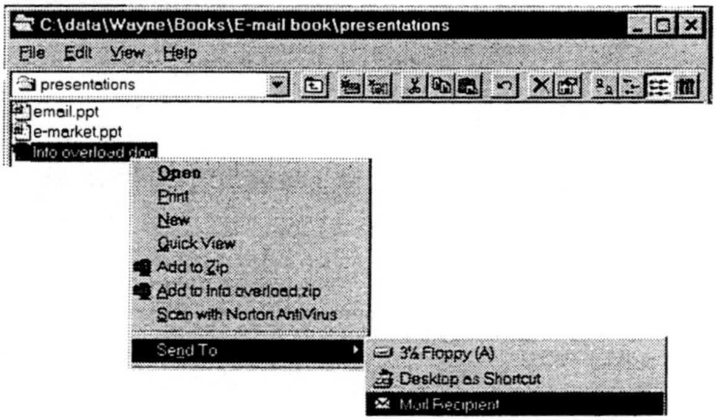

Figure 1-3.5

TIP: When browsing your hard disk for files using windows 95, try using your right mouse button to select a document you want to send to someone. Your E-mail software may allow you to automatically create a new message with the document attached.

Sometimes E-mail systems do not work

A variety of technical problems can prevent you from receiving messages. Your corporate E-mail system may experience occasional problems, but Internet E-mail is a best-effort delivery system. No one person, company or organization can be held accountable for lost messages. Think carefully about whether you want to rely on E-mail for critical information.

Here is an example where I regret having relied on Internet E-mail. I got an opportunity to travel to Europe on business. I was asked to go at the last minute. The organizer was to send me information about the travel arrangements by E-mail, including the departure date and my airline and hotel arrangements.

On the day that I was to receive this information, my E-mail service provider closed my account. My credit card expiry date had come and gone and I had forgotten to notify the service provider of the new date. Rather than contacting me and saying, "We have a problem with your credit card. Could you kindly verify that this information is correct?", they closed my E-mail account.

I should have requested that the travel information be sent to me through a more dependable channel.

Large attachments can prolong connect-time

Zip up or compress large attachments before sending them. This does not happen automatically. There are many utilities on the market, but WinZip is my personal favorite.

If I receive a large attachment that I didn't expect, the five-minute job to check my E-mail may turn into a lengthy procedure that I am afraid to cancel until the entire download is finished. I may not even have any indication how large that attachment is and how long it will take until it is done.

Use another way to distribute attachments, or ask permission before sending, particularly if the item is just for general interest. If the attachment is for multiple recipients, store the information on a central file server instead.

Software can contain glitches and bugs

Before you buy any new program, especially if you've got E-mail-enabled applications, be sure to test compatibility before upgrading. If you're going to upgrade to the next version of that word processor or you're going to add a new scheduling program, make sure that it doesn't interfere with your E-mail system or vice versa. Always perform a backup of the system before installing anything new. You may want to go back to your old settings.

Too much junk can clog your system

E-mail messages accumulate more quickly than most people think. Get into the habit of deleting messages frequently, especially those containing attachments. Hard disks fill up quickly, and if yours does, your computer or E-mail server could crash. In a corporate environment, someone watches over the servers. If you are on your own... you're on your own.

In many corporate environments, the E-mail administrator imposes a limit on the volume of messages that a user may store. Learn what your limit is and find alternate ways to archive your information. One way is to copy old messages off the mail server and onto your hard disk. Be sure to back up this data if it is no longer on the corporate server. You are probably responsible for your own hard disk. Other alternatives include storing only the necessary project information in a Personal Information Manager (PIM) or project-tracking database. Also, don't forget that floppy disks can be used for off-line storage, and many mail systems allow you to save messages as text files.

Clean up the leftovers

Your E-mail system might keep a copy of messages that you send. I find this feature useful. Many times someone else asks a question that I have already answered. I can quickly go back to a previously-sent message and re-send it as a new message. Others prefer not to use this feature, and will turn it off if that is an option.

Your system may also keep a folder of deleted messages (just in case you ever didn't really want to delete a message). Be sure to empty that folder frequently, particularly if you have sent or deleted many messages containing attachments.

Chapter 1-4

E-mail Privacy and Security

What risk does E-mail bring to mind? Privacy. Information can leak in other ways, but people fear the electronic channels the most. Although the concern is justified, it is primarily the fear of the unknown that gives E-mail a bad name.

How likely is it that you will be attacked? That depends largely on who you are and what you do. For the average person with an average income who communicates mainly with friends, the risk is not that high. But become a public figure and your risk increases.

E-mail, like any recorded communication, places information at risk. In fact, anytime communication is recorded, it can be reviewed later by someone other than the original participants.

Defend your personal privacy

If you contribute regularly to public discussions on the Internet, you may be giving up a degree of personal security because your habits may be tracked. Take newsgroups as an example. Newsgroups are public forums for discussing areas of interest, and topics range from raising pets to bestiality, from education to anarchy. DejaNews is an Internet search engine that collects old newsgroup discussions. Search for a topic of interest and you will find a newsgroup archive of your topic. You can even read the authors' names, and then view profiles about the authors that include the names of other newsgroups they have contributed to, regardless of how unflattering this information may be!

DajaNews can be found at http://www.dejanews.com.

Kids—don't talk to strangers!

We tell our children at an early age not to talk to strangers, but what does a stranger look like? Children are easily influenced, and are perhaps too trusting. Don't let you or your children become victims of a predator trolling on-line for impressionable people to prey on.

Has our society become overly paranoid? Are we too protective? Friends of mine came to visit, and shocked my neighbors by letting their kids go to the park alone. What happened to the days when your only concern was that the kids were home for dinner? Many people believe that living near a highway puts a family at a higher risk because more people pass near the house. What then about the information highway passing through the home?

Only you can choose the appropriate level of concern for your family. Here are some guidelines.

- Ask your children to introduce you to their new on-line friends.
- Ask if you may review their sent messages.
- Train family members to conceal personal information such as where they live or go to school.

Consider installing software that can track your child's activities: Cybersnoop from Pearl Software (www.pearlsw.com) lets you record and monitor what your children have been up to. Visit my resource page for an up-to-date list of tools (http://www.ITcoach.com).

Saved E-mail messages can be read by others

Messages that are saved may be read, so make sure that any information you receive is stored securely. You also want to make sure that the people you send information to do not put you in jeopardy by storing your messages improperly. During the Persian Gulf War in 1991 a U.S. commander's laptop was stolen from his jeep. Fortunately, when the person who took the computer realized that it contained sensitive information, he decided to return it anonymously with a note saying, "I am a thief, not a traitor." But think of the result if that information had fallen into the wrong hands.

If your mail messages are saved on your hard drive, you are responsible to protect them. Some E-mail programs allow you to encrypt or password-protect those files. Be aware, though, that if you forget your password no-one will be able to help you retrieve the files you have saved.

If you leave your E-mail application open when you are away from your desk, anyone can read your mail. If you share a computer with others, they might not realize that you are logged on, and end up reading your messages thinking that they are theirs. This frequently happens when a group of people share a computer connected to the Internet.

The Internet browser software has a built-in E-mail client. The client must be configured with an E-mail account. It is common for someone to enter their account information and forget to change it after they have finished checking their mail. The next person that uses the system will end up sending all of their messages from your account and reading the contents of your in-box if the account information remains unchanged.

WARNING: Don't forget to remove messages from your "sent mail" and "deleted items" folders before you leave a shared system.

Someone might eavesdrop in your office

Someone can eavesdrop on an E-mail conversation just as they can on a spoken one. A visitor to your office might inadvertently look over your shoulder at the computer, or see the screen when they walk into your empty office.

To protect your confidential information, log out of your E-mail application when you leave your desk, or run a password-protected screen saver.

Beware of electronic eavesdroppers

Sent messages can also be intercepted during transmission by someone with a few simple tools. Think of E-mail as an electronic postcard. If you require better security, use a different method of communicating or make use of security tools to encrypt the message.

Countries have various laws relating to the encryption technology that individuals may use. The governments of many countries reserve the right to break into any communication medium they deem necessary. If you export certain encryption technologies from the U.S. you may be breaking the law. By importing certain technologies into France, you also break the law.

Your messages are stored on others' servers

E-mail leaves a written record. Something you write might come back in the future to incriminate you. A message could be taken out of context when reviewed at a later date. Be aware that when you transmit E-mail messages, they don't simply arrive at the other person's computer. They are first stored on a server somewhere on the network, and from that server they get forwarded to a second server then possibly a third and a fourth until eventually they arrive.

E-mail servers are backed up every night so that in the event of a system failure messages can be recovered and transmitted once the system has been repaired. The backup tapes are often archived to provide a way of recovering old messages that never arrived.

During the Oliver North trial in the United States in the mid-1990s, E-mail messages recovered from backup tapes were admitted as evidence. Some people delete absolutely every E-mail message they receive so that the information cannot be taken out of context and used later. In many cases that information still sits on a tape somewhere.

WARNING: Your organization may have a legal obligation to archive records. See your lawyer or records manager to determine if you can legally delete E-mail messages.

Is your E-mail administrator your best friend?

As a business professional you know your job very well, but do you find yourself out of your element when it comes to computers? Fortunately, your company hired someone to take care of the computer systems and you. But just where does this system administrator fit in your corporate hierarchy? They must be fairly high up because most companies and individual users trust them with access to all of their corporate data.

In a secure environment, the administrator should not know your password. It unlocks your mailbox and provides access to all of your messages. Even if the security of your in-box doesn't concern you, perhaps it concerns the CEO who just sent you a copy of the preliminary financial report for your review.

The administrator should be able to help you if you forget your password. The best systems will not allow anyone to find your old password, but a new one can be generated. The generation of passwords on a secure system is an auditable event, meaning that if a security audit was performed, the person who changed the password could be identified.

Who breaks into E-mail?

These hackers may be your competitors looking to gain an edge by any means. They may be teenagers who thrill to the challenge of successfully infiltrating a company's computer system, with bragging rights the booty. It may be a vigilante consumer who feels your company has wronged them in some way. Or it may be a modern-day Billy the Kid, robbing the electronic stagecoach filled with credit card information.

You can protect yourself from electronic robbery

We are comfortable providing our credit card numbers over the telephone, but fear entering them in a computer. An eavesdropper can easily steal our numbers either way. With relatively simple tools one can collect electronic data and with a computer program sort through to identify useful information. Ask yourself, "How likely am I to be targeted?"

To protect you, tools exist that allow the sender to encrypt information so that only a receiver with the correct code can unlock the message and view its contents. These encryption tools are getting easier to use and are a necessary component in E-commerce —electronic banking and retailing.

Secure your corporation

Trade secrets and business opportunities are the primary break-in targets in corporations, although smear campaigns against companies whose practices are considered unethical do occur.

Financial information that could provide an advantage on the stock market is also worth stealing.

Vigilante consumers attack via E-mail!

One of the favorite ways to electronically attack a corporation is to throw so much traffic at it that its E-mail system is brought to its knees. This hate mail is known as "flaming" or "letter bombs," and its intent is to disrupt the normal flow of information. In the short term, not much can be done to stop these repeated messages other than hope your system is up to the challenge. If the attack persists, an electronic firewall can be configured to deny all traffic from a specific sender's address. The craftiest attacker will skirt the firewall by sending their letter bombs from other people's E-mail servers.

Espionage and sabotage

In today's information-heavy world, knowledge is power. A company that knows more than its competitors has a business advantage. In warfare, the more information you have about your enemy's strengths, weaknesses and position, the stronger you are. And the better the quality of information, the stronger a weapon it is.

Sending out false information under a competitor's name is an equally powerful sabotage strategy, capable of creating mistrust in the legitimate messages that company sends. For example, an electronic impersonator disguised as your company's president could distribute inaccurate information about the financial state of your organization.

Documents can be forged

Incoming messages may not be from who you think they are. I could impersonate someone and how would you know? Imagine how you could damage someone's reputation by using their E-mail account to send messages, rude or otherwise. For electronic commerce to work, the sender must be verifiable; likewise for legal documents transmitted electronically. Many countries have policies relating to the use of "digital signatures" to verify the sender.

Digital signatures or "authentication certificates" allow the recipient to check if the message was really sent by the person whose name is on the message. See Part 5 of this book for more details.

E-mail attachments can contain viruses

Viruses have been a menace since the early days of the personal computer. The most common type of virus is a small program that imbeds itself in another computer program. When the infected program is run, the virus does its damage.

E-mail is one more means of distributing viruses. Infected programs can be sent as E-mail attachments. The trick is to convince the recipient to open the attachment and launch the infected program. Jokes and games are often used as Trojan horses to get viruses into your computer.

With the Word macro virus, word processing documents can now be infected and are much easier to convince the victim to run. Usually these documents come from someone you know: the virus is on their computer and they have inadvertently infected the document they sent to you.

It is best to save attachments to disk before opening them, and scan for viruses using a commercial virus-checker. Some E-mail systems can scan messages' contents for viruses as the messages arrive.

Beware of the human E-mail virus!

A part of your computer can be programmed by even the most primitive hacker to automatically generate huge amounts of E-mail traffic. This part can usually be found between the keyboard and the chair back—it is the user. It all starts with a hoax message that could cause enough congestion to strangle an E-mail system if everyone forwards it to everyone else.

Example:

```
Subject: virus warning
>Date: Monday, 09 March, 1998 8:29AM
>
>
>
>If you receive an E-mail titled "WIN A HOLIDAY"
>DO NOT open it. It will erase everything on your
>hard drive. Forward this letter out to as many
>people as you can. This is a new, very malicious
>virus and not many people know about it.
```

```
>
>please share it with everyone that might access
>the Internet. Once again, pass this along to
>EVERYONE in your address book so that this may be
>stopped.
>Also, do not open or even look at any mail that
>says "RETURNED OR UNABLE TO DELIVER." This virus
>will attach itself to your computer components
>and render them useless. Immediately delete any
>mail items that say this. AOL has said that this
>is a very dangerous virus and that there is NO
>remedy for it at this time.
>Please practice cautionary measures and forward
>this to all your online friends ASAP.
```

The bottom line is this: E-mail messages are harmless text documents. The E-mail message itself cannot contain a virus, although attachments can. If you fear viruses, suspect your attachments, not your plain-text documents and E-mail messages.

But sadly this will not always be the case in the future. As E-mail programs begin to support E-mail messages formatted using Hypertext Markup Language (HTML), your next message could appear to you as a Web page. Web pages *can* contain malicious scripts.

Visit my web site for the latest information on E-mail viruses: http//www.ITcoach.com

Chapter 1-5

Other Risks

Security risks are not the only problems in electronic communications. As you become more and more dependent on E-mail, any event that prevents you from receiving a message could hamper your work. Likewise, what the recipients of your messages do with that mail could have an impact on you. And finally, if you overuse E-mail you can damage your productivity and your well-being. This chapter contains examples of problems you should be aware of.

Being spammed to death

Unethical advertisers who distribute to huge mailing lists might use your E-mail mail system to disseminate their information. Very high volume can bog down your system. Sometimes this is the intentional work of a malicious individual. It's like the kind of havoc we've seen Greenpeace create by putting their little boats in the way of a whaling ship. Electronic warfare is a tactic that enemies can use against you or your company.

Messages can get lost en route

E-mail messages sent across the Internet or even in an internal network don't always reach their destination. They can be lost during transmission because of a communication line problem. They can be lost while stored temporarily on a server that crashes without back-up. Most E-mail systems can keep track of lost messages and re-send them, but you should also have some checks and balances in place. If you need to E-mail urgent information, keep a copy of what you send. Follow up to make sure it arrived safely.

Allow for the possibility of down time

Boats always fail on the nicest days of the summer, snowblowers have problems starting only on mornings of deep snow, and computer systems crash when you are in a hurry.

Down time at a critical moment can destroy your business. Remember my story in Chapter 1-3 ("Technology Problems") about my European trip? I didn't receive my last-minute travel information because my E-mail service provider suddenly closed my account when my credit card expired. Then they said I would not have service again until the next billing cycle—a month away. (So I changed service providers.) Be sure that your service provider considers your E-mail connection to be as important as you do.

Oh, no! I sent that message to the wrong person!

With the click of a button you can mistakenly send information to the wrong address. For example, if you receive a copy of an E-mail message, you might try to respond to the sender but accidentally respond to the entire circulation list. Always double-check the "Send To" and the "Cc" line of your message before pressing "send."

An associate told me that he once accidentally faxed a client proposal to his supplier and the supplier's contract to the client. He didn't get the job—perhaps the client saw his markup on services and shopped for a better deal.

The following is a situation that happened on the phone but could just as easily happen using E-mail.

I once received an odd voice mail unknowingly left by two friends of mine. One called my number and received my voice mail. Not wanting to leave a message, he quickly hung up and dialed the next number. His phone system supported three-way calling, or conference calls, and he actually placed my voice mail on hold by lifting the receiver too soon after hanging up. When the second person answered the call, a three-way conference call was started. The entire conversation was recorded by my voice mail system unbeknownst to them. The point is that depending on who the callers were and what was discussed, this technical glitch could have had serious ramifications. Accidentally responding to all E-mail recipients can have the same effect.

E-mail can't keep a secret

When you send a confidential message, make it clear that you do not wish that information to be passed on. Better yet, assume everything will be passed on, and decide if E-mail is the most suitable means to communicate that message.

Pasted messages can put words in your mouth

It is easy to take a message that you receive and forward it to someone else with your comments attached. If you forward a message along with your comments, don't mix your words with those of the original sender. Make it clear who said what and in what context, or else your words may be attributed to the originating author. In the example below, Bob has forwarded a message to me from Fred, his CEO. By not clearly identifying which comments are his and which ones are from Fred's original message, he has left the impression that it is Fred who feels that sponsoring my race team would be a good idea. What Bob should have done is to have composed a new message, and marked ">" in the left margin of each line of text that was copied from Fred's original message.

Example:

```
TO: Wayne
FROM: Bob

Hi Wayne,

Just thought I would forward this bit of
information to you.

**Original message sent by CEO Fred**
Past-quarter earnings show that the company is
once again profitable. We have exceeded all
expectations and are set for a banner year.

Wayne, I propose that we take at least half of
our profits from last quarter and fund your
race team. The sponsorship exposure could help
us recruit new staff.
```

In Bob's message, is it clear to you that Bob and not the CEO is proposing sponsorship?

(Bob, by the way, has no authority to make decisions, but is a big motorsports fan.)

E-mail can be addictive

For some reason, E-mail has an addiction quality. Like waiting for a letter from a sweetheart or pen pal, it is easy to become caught up in an E-mail conversation, eagerly awaiting each reaction to your last comment.

You can waste a lot of time by continually jumping from your work to check your E-mail. Whether you see this as interrupting yourself or as E-mail interrupting you, be aware of the distraction of too-frequent E-mail checking, especially if you work in the isolation of a home office. See Part 3 of this book, "Stop being a Slave to E-mail," for solutions.

Beware of burning out

All too common today are the mental health risks associated with information overload, overstress and burnout. E-mail contributes to that load. I know many people who receive hundreds of E-mail messages a day. They can become overwhelmed. For those suffering from burnout, take a holiday and then check out Part 3 of this book: "Stop Being a Slave to E-mail."

Part II

Communicating Effectively

Chapter 2-1

Writing with the Right Meaning

Many people do not take the time to think about how their message will be perceived by the recipient.

But there is one writing style suitable for electronic chat with a pen pal, and another for composing a message to the CEO of your company (unless he or she is your best buddy).

In this chapter I will focus on some of little things in your message that can confuse your readers at best, and anger them at worst.

DO NOT WRITE USING ALL CAPITAL LETTERS!

Avoid writing your E-mail messages in capital letters. It gives the readers the impression that you are shouting at them.

A number of years ago I managed a group of technical consultants. One of them was a stereotype techie propeller-head genius. He was a whiz with computers but not a very good communicator.

He often sent me E-mail that distressed me. The way the words appeared on my screen emphasized a negative side to the message that was not intended.

Example:

"WAYNE - YOU ALWAYS WANT ME TO PROVIDE WEEKLY STATUS REPORTS AND I NEVER HAVE TIME TO WRITE THEM. DON'T YOU THINK THAT ONE A MONTH IS ENOUGH?"

The message in this example gave me the impression that he was angry with me, and that I was unreasonable for expecting regular status reports. I almost responded with:

NO, I DON'T THINK ONCE A MONTH IS ENOUGH!!! JUST DO IT.

For some reason, sentences written in capital letters seem to attack the reader, regardless of the words used. Capital letters seem harsh in a sentence. Compare the first example to the one below.

```
"Wayne - You always want me to provide weekly
status reports and I never have time to write
them. Don't you think one a month is enough?"
```

When I walked over to his desk to find out why he was so angry with me, I discovered a smiling, likable employee who loved his job and was brimming with enthusiasm. He had just calculated the time it took to complete a status report, and he had a wonderful idea how he could make the company more profitable by reducing the number of status reports and using the extra time to work on billable projects.

Can you imagine what it would have done for employee moral if I had sent a message back based on my initial response?

Avoid starting sentences with pronouns

When the message in the example above is re-written in lower case, it no longer shouts at me, but it still seems to attack. By removing "You always" or "You never," a sentence can easily be re-worded to ask a question or present an idea in a positive fashion.

Example:

```
Hi Wayne,
Are monthly status reports enough? I can be more
productive with the time I save.
```

Punctuation to emphasize a word or thought

To further ensure that the important part of your message is understood, you can highlight key words or phrases, as in the following example.

Example:

```
Hi Wayne,
Are monthly status reports enough?
I can be MORE productive.
I could use the time I save to do BILLABLE work!
```

Alternately, some people emphasize a word by placing it in quotation marks or between other symbols:

I can be more "productive."

I can be more **productive.**

Use emoticons to add tone to your message

Emoticons are icons or pictures used to depict emotion.

Before you begin using emoticons be aware that not everyone appreciates their use. Some see it as juvenile and unbusinesslike. There are very few places where a smiley face can cause anger, but for some people E-mail is one.

To those people I say LOOSEN UP! <grin>.

The idea is to create a picture using only the standard characters available on your keyboard, since all E-mail systems can support these in a message. (Turn you head sideways to the left if you are having difficulty seeing the faces.)

:-)	smiley face
;-)	mischievous face
:-(	sad face
:-0	shock or disbelief

Hope this helps. ☺

FYI: here are some useful abbreviations

You may also come across some of the following abbreviations in E-mail messages, particularly in Internet newsgroups. Be aware that not everyone understands their meanings. In a *Dilbert* newsletter I received, Scott Adams told of a co-worker who thought Adams was angry whenever he used "FYI."

BTW	By the way
FYI	For your information
FAQ	Frequently Asked Questions
IMHO	In my humble opinion
FWIW	For what it's worth
RTFM	Read the fine manual

Making a good impression

Finally, don't forget that the first, and perhaps only, impression that some people will get of you is through your E-mail correspondence. While brief messages are appreciated, good English is still important. Many managers and executives choose to not waste their time reading incomprehensible messages.

To help you with your writing style I asked noted business-writing expert Dr. Julie Miller to provide a few tips from her book *Business Writing That Counts! How to write quickly and clearly in three easy steps.*

C.L.E.V.R. solutions to your business-writing concerns

A thought from Dr. Julie:

> "Use these tips along with a good dose of common sense. Remember, everything in moderation. Your goal is productivity, not perfectionism."

C stands for Clarity

L stands for Language

E stands for Economy

V stands for Variety

R stands for Rules

Clarity is the essence of good writing. Expressing exactly what you mean *is* clear writing *and* clear thinking.

- ◊ Be concise. Include specifics— time, place, numbers or names.
- ◊ Simplify your writing.
- ◊ Say NO! to the passive voice. That is, don't say, "The meeting room will be booked tomorrow, and the schedule must be adhered to." Say, "Martha will book the meeting room tomorrow, and all members of the committee must adhere to the schedule."

  As Dr. Julie says, "The pressure of time is not an excuse for unclear or confusing writing. *AND* it could cost your business money, time, energy, prestige, and even a lawsuit!"

Language should be tailored to each specific audience. Use strong, concrete nouns, or use metaphors and analogies to make your point clear.

- ◊ Avoid clichés.
- ◊ Avoid jargon when you can, and define it when you can't.
- ◊ Avoid sexism.

  Dr. Julie says, "Vague, ambiguous language that contains clichés, acronyms or jargon can deceive, confuse, and even irritate the reader." Remember who your audience is!

Economical writing shows consideration for the reader's time. Be brief but informative. Provide an appropriate amount of detail but make every word count.

- ◊ Keep your sentences shorter than 20 words.
- ◊ Use one- and two-syllable words. Shorten words where possible.
- ◊ Keep paragraphs brief, with one idea per paragraph.

  Dr. Julie says, "Don't waste the reader's time. Get to the point!"

Variety makes your writing interesting. Use a mix of short and long sentences to make your writing sound more like a conversation. Don't make the reader work too hard, and don't put him or her to sleep.

- ◊ Ask a question.
- ◊ Use quotations.
- ◊ Use punctuation to add punch!

Dr. Julie says, "One idea can be expressed many ways. Choose sentences that keep your reader alert."

Rules can get in the way of getting organized and getting started. Some rules can be broken and others cannot, but let common sense be your guide. Choose the wording that will get your message across most effectively.

- ◊ Use a positive tone.
- ◊ Mind your manners. Please be courteous, and say thank you.
- ◊ Be personable. You are an important part of your writing.

Dr. Julie says, "It used to be an unforgivable sin to write sentence fragments. No more! Fragments are incomplete sentences and in certain circumstances work wonderfully. See you soon!"

A note from Dr. Julie:

```
To:          You, the Reader
From:        Julie Miller
[Julie@DrJulieMiller.com]
Subject:     Business Writing that Counts

      If you are uncertain about your own
      words, visit my Web site for more
      useful tips.

      - - - - - - - - - - - - - - - -
      Dr. Julie Miller
      BUSINESS WRITING THAT COUNTS!
      http://www.DrJulieMiller.com
      15401 NE 177th Drive
      Woodinville, WA 98072
      (425) 485-3221 Office
      (425) 481-3197 Fax
      - - - - - - - - - - - - - - - -
```

Chapter 2-2

Attracting the Reader with Attractive Messages

Make your content pretty yet readable

Much to my surprise, one of the questions I hear most frequently is how to make an E-mail message stand out. How do you make it more attractive? How do you catch the reader's eye?

My short answer is that readers are more attracted to short, concise E-mail than to a long, drawn-out message regardless of how it is formatted.

That said, there are tricks you can use to add some splash to your message.

Corporate E-mail systems have lots of formatting features

Unlike Internet E-mail, the proprietary messaging systems used by most corporate employees are feature-rich. Composing a message using Microsoft Exchange, Novell's GroupWise, and most of the other popular E-mail systems, is like using a word processor.

Sample E-mail Message:

```
To:       You, The Reader
From:     Wayne, The ITcoach
Subject:  formatting messages
```

Headings can be bold

Though I prefer to break separate topics into individual messages, bold headings are an effective way to separate different topics within your message.

- Bullets can be used to identify important points.
- Detail can be included later in the message.
- Paragraphs can be indented.
- Charts and graphs can be included.

Important words can be *emphasized* using *italics* or **bold-face.**

Other important things you should know about your corporate E-mail system:

Attachments -	You can add graphs, charts, pictures and documents to your message. With most systems, these can either be included in the message body or added as an attachment, or you can place a link in the message. Remember that an attachment is sent to every recipient of the message, while a link is simply a reference point back to the original document, stored centrally on the server. For a link to function, the recipient must be connected to your network and have access to the files that you have linked to. Links can save storage space and reduce the load on your network. Also, if the linked document's contents change, you do not have to send a new message to update your recipients. Be aware that linked documents are not available to people who read their messages off-line, until they re-connect.
Gateways -	A gateway is a connection between two dissimilar E-mail systems. When your message leaves your corporate system and travels on to the Internet, the message must pass through a gateway where it is converted to the Internet mail format. When you send messages to another system: ♦ attachments can be lost. ♦ links will not work. ♦ formatting may be lost or unreadable.

You can format Internet mail messages, too

Internet mail has traditionally contained only plain text. You have few tools at hand to enhance the appearance of a text message, but here are some examples of what you *can* do:

```
CAPITAL LETTERS CAN BE USED FOR HEADINGS

Leading spaces can be added to indent a line

-Special characters can be used as bullets,

Or for underlining.
-------------------


       ====================================
       Text boxes can be drawn using = sign
       ====================================


       You can even draw pictures!
```

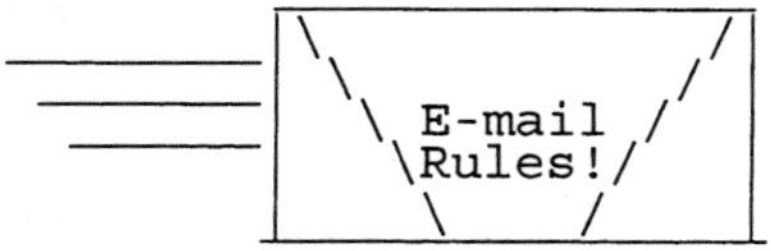

While *any* E-mail system will be able to deliver your message intact if you stick to plain text, consider that the process of converting from one system to another may introduce extra spaces or characters that may mess up the alignment of text in your document.

- If you draw pictures, keep them small.
- Send a test message to someone else to see how it looks.
- The message may be displayed differently on different systems.

Enhanced formatting is now available for Internet mail

A new feature of many E-mail programs is the ability to compose, send and receive *Hypertext Markup Language* documents (HTML). HTML is the language understood by Internet Web browsers and some E-mail programs.

If your E-mail client supports this feature, essentially you are sending a Web page to your recipient. Unless you include pictures, Web pages are just simple text with certain text patterns recognized as control codes for formatting.

While this feature is a great enhancement to Internet E-mail, the majority of Internet mail users may not be using a compatible E-mail client that supports this feature. My advice is that unless you and the recipient have agreed to exchange HTML messages, stick to plain text.

The following is an example of an E-mail message I received while writing this book

Unfortunately for the sender, my E-mail client did not recognize HTML text. So, this is how the message appeared when I tried to read it.

```
<HTML><BODY>

<P><FONT FACE = "Arial" COLOR = "#000000" SIZE =
"3">Just published -- "Slash Your Rent: A
Commercial Tenant's Explicit Guide"
<P>The Knowledge to Save You Serious Rent $$.
<FONT FACE = "Times New Roman" COLOR = "#000000"
SIZE = "5">Please go to <FONT FACE = "Times New
Roman" COLOR = "#0000FF" SIZE =
"5"><U>http://www.comles.qpg.com</U><FONT FACE =
"Times New Roman" COLOR = "#0000FF" SIZE = "5">
</BODY></HTML>
```

If you receive an HTML E-mail message that you are unable to read, copy the text or save it to a text file with the extension .htm (sample.htm, for example). Now you can open this document in your Web browser to see how it was meant to look.

This is what that message said:

> Just published — "Slash Your Rent: A Commercial Tenant's Explicit Guide"
>
> The Knowledge to Save You Serious Rent $$. Please go to http://www.comles.qpg.com

Use attachments to spruce up your message

If your E-mail system limits how you can format your message, why not use your word processor to create a document and attach the document to your message?

Why you should use attachments:

- Take advantage of the feature-rich formatting capabilities of your word processor and other applications.
- Ensure that the message looks correct when it is read.
- The attached document can be printed, read and modified. This is very useful if the content is a report or other work in progress.

Why you should not use attachments:

- Attachments can be lost when sent between dissimilar E-mail systems.
- The recipient may not have access to the application (e.g. Microsoft Word) that you used to create the attachment.
- Attachments are usually much larger than the same text included in a simple mail message.
- The recipient must take extra steps to read an attached document.

Consider an attachment to be an extra to your message. Unless you know for certain that everyone on your distribution list can read the "features" and attachments that you use, make sure that your message can stand on its own. The attachment might not arrive, but your message will.

If you want to make your Internet mail more attractive, programs like ActiveMail will help you convert your formatted documents and pictures into a *Graphics Interchange Format* (GIF) file that can be sent via E-mail and read by anyone with a Web browser or compatible E-mail client.

ActiveMail is available on the Internet at:
http://www.spco.com/Store/products/activemail.html

Or, if you prefer, send video messages using CVideo-Mail by Cubic Video Comm http://www.Cvideo.com

You can also dictate your E-mail messages with Voice E-mail from Wizard Software http://www.wizardsoftware.com

Chapter 2-3

Finding the Right Address

You can't tell the players without a scorecard

Before you can send E-mail to someone, you need their E-mail address. Unfortunately, there is no official group with the responsibility of maintaining a list of E-mail addresses the way that telephone companies maintain telephone directories.

For Internet mail, there are a number of search engines that you can check to find an E-mail address, and your own organization may have a company-wide directory. Many companies, however, do not, especially if they use a variety of E-mail systems across the organization. For instance, Accounting may be on the corporate E-mail system, but Engineering and Sales may have their own, and each from different vendors.

Since most proprietary E-mail systems cannot communicate directly with each other, it is difficult to create a central E-mail directory. Furthermore, some companies guard their address list very closely.

Years ago I worked on a project with a large organization and asked if we could communicate using E-mail. Both my company and theirs had the same internal E-mail system, so connecting the two would have been a breeze. (The Internet had not yet gained the popularity it has today.)

When I asked if we could connect, the answer I got was, "Oh, no, we can't do that—you might start sending E-mail to our president."

LDAP is coming to the rescue

A new solution is emerging to allow E-mail systems to share address lists more easily. "Lightweight Directory Access Protocol" (LDAP) is a standard for sharing or publishing E-mail address books.

Once E-mail systems and E-mail clients are all LDAP-compliant, you will be able to query any E-mail system that you have been given access to. As standards continue to evolve, all E-mail systems will easily exchange address lists. Through public directories and company directories (both private and public) you will easily be able to find the address you need.

Try the Web

Many organizations now include their address books on their Internet Web sites (either publicly for all to see or privately for their employees on the road). Organizations that are concerned about junk mail or security may choose not to publish their addresses.

If someone sends me an E-mail message asking for my consulting services, I find out as much about their company as I can in order to prepare. Before our next conversation I visit their Web site.

What if you don't know their Web address?

If you do not know someone's Web address, but you do know their E-mail address, try using the "domain name" portion of their E-mail address. The domain name uniquely identifies a company's location on the Internet.

For example, if you receive a message from "info@ITcoach.com," you can try the Web address http://www.ITcoach.com to locate the Web site. Using this educated guess you can locate many Web sites.

Ask for an E-mail address when you gather contact information

If you are trying to contact your friend in XYZ company, why not try the easy method—call and ask for the E-mail address. You could also look at their Web site, if they have one; you might find a corporate directory. You could search in an Internet directory, too.

E-mail addresses are so common today that a large percentage of people you meet will have one. Get in the habit of asking for this vital piece of information, and don't forget to ask them how often they check their mail. You want to know if E-mail is an appropriate method of contacting them.

Here is a list of a few Internet E-mail directories to help in your search:

AOL netfind	http://www.aol.com/netfind/person.html
whowhere	http://www.whowhere.com/
switchboard	http://www.switchboard.com/
555-1212.com	http://www.555-1212.com/
bigfoot	http://www.bigfoot.com/
four11.com	http://www.four11.com/

Internet—The universally accepted E-mail address

If you are familiar with Internet mail you are used to seeing an address like mine: info@ITcoach.com. But not all E-mail systems follow the Internet standard. Proprietary systems such as Microsoft Mail, Novell GroupWise or CC Mail, Beyond Mail and Microsoft Exchange require a gateway to translate incoming and outgoing Internet messages. Fortunately, these companies recognize the importance of Internet E-mail access so they provide gateways.

In order to exchange messages with other systems, you will have multiple E-mail addresses that conform to the standard for each mail system yours is connected to.

The gateway not only translates the message into the proper form but also keeps track of the multiple versions of your address.

Regardless of which internal mail system your company uses, for the outside world to contact you through your company's

Internet mail connection, put your Internet mail address on your business card.

Put your E-mail address on your business card

Many studies have found that E-mail is becoming the way that people prefer to communicate for business. With today's hectic schedules it is far more likely that you will get someone's voice mail than actually get them on the telephone. You will probably have to leave a message anyway, so you, and many others, prefer to leave E-mail.

How are Internet mail addresses composed?

The Internet is made up of many computer networks and subnetworks. Each group of networks owned by a given company is referred to as a "domain." Domain names are allocated based on type of organization or location. The Internet evolved in the United States so many of the top-level domains are US-specific. The .com domain, though, is internationally used.

American and General Domains

.com	commercial
.edu	educational (colleges and Universities)
.gov	US government organizations
.int	international organizations
.mil	US military groups
.net	network resellers and other network organizations
.org	non-profit organizations

Geographical Country Codes

As the Internet became a public entity, other countries created their own top-level domains.

In Canada, companies that have offices or presence in more than one province can register their domain under the Canadian ".ca" domain. If they operate in only one province, their domain name can be registered as a subdomain of their province.

When I registered my domain name, I could have used *ITcoach.on.ca* since my office is in Ontario, Canada. But I chose *ITcoach.com* to reflect the international nature of my business.

If you know the domain name of an organization, and know the naming convention that they use to create mailboxes, then it is easy to decode their Internet E-mail address.

Example:

Transport Canada is a government department in Canada.

"Some Person" at Transport Canada would be PersoS@tc.gc.ca

.ca	Canada	
.gc	Government of Canada	(a sub-domain of Canada)
.tc	Transport Canada	(a sub-domain of Government of Canada)

Other countries have their own country codes. *Here are a few examples:*

.au Australia

.uk United Kingdom

.fr France

A complete list can be found at http://www.internic.net

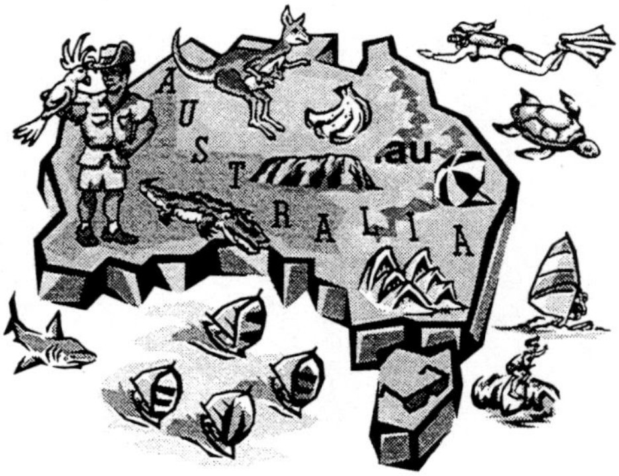

Part III

Stop Being a Slave to E-mail

Chapter 3-1

Manage Your In-box

Most people have a hard enough time managing the stacks of paper on their desk, let alone the piles of information in their computers. I recently moved to a house with a two-car garage because I needed more space. I still can't park a car inside! The amount of junk you will collect is directly proportional to the space available. Computers encourage us to keep more information than we otherwise might. One colleague of mine figures that it is cheaper to buy a bigger hard drive than to take the time to delete old files and messages!

Why delete messages?

In a corporate environment, your E-mail administrator will not like you very much if your messages remain undeleted on the E-mail server. With the first version of Microsoft Exchange server released in 1996, the physical limit for the message store was 16 gigabytes (that's the equivalent of almost 12,000 floppy disks). Only two short years later this limit had to be increased. The point is that if everyone left their junk on the server, it could soon fill up and would be unable to receive new messages.

A second reason for keeping the number of stored messages to a minimum is to save time. If you have to sort through hundreds of messages every time you look for information, your search will not be very efficient. Stored messages often become redundant once you receive a more recent message.

Finally, the more you surround yourself with clutter, the higher your stress level will be. It is easier to clean things up as you go along than to face the daunting task of tackling a mountain of unsorted messages.

E-mail began as a tool for sending brief messages. It has become a strategic business tool for many organizations. As a result, E-mail is now being used to transmit more material, and more important material too. Information storage strategies are changing as a result. Check with your E-mail administrator for company guidelines.

Move your mail messages to your own hard disk

To eliminate the possibility that your E-mail server will fill up, the system administrator may impose a limit on the size of each user's mailbox. Find out the limits in your system, if any, and consider what you will do if you approach those limits. Depending on your type of system, you may be able to move your messages to a file on your own hard disk, or a floppy disk.

If you are in a corporate environment and you decide to store your messages locally rather than on the E-mail server, be aware that you and you alone are responsible to back up those files. Store critical information on floppy disks as a precaution, or as a permanent archive. They are cheap, so use one per project if necessary.

Should you read your mail in the morning?

By getting an early start, you can arrive at work relaxed and ready to take on the day. Spend your first quiet moments before the day piles up doing the important things—plan your day before the hectic pace takes over. Don't be driven by interruptions. Deal with the most important things first.

For some people an efficient start includes checking their E-mail. Perhaps your daily plan depends on the E-mail you receive. Depending on the nature of your work, you may check E-mail once at the start of the day, or only after all of your other important tasks are complete.

Your answer will depend greatly on how strategic E-mail is to your job function. If you are in a support role and your E-mail might tell you that you have a fire to put out, then by all means make checking your E-mail a morning priority. But don't waste your most productive time of the day checking discretionary messages. Focus on the important ones at the time when they need your attention.

The three-step approach to responding to your E-mail

Dave Songco recently retired as the Assistant Director of the computer division at the National Institutes of Health. Like many managers and executives, during his tenure he received many thousands of E-mail messages, sometimes hundreds a day. A master at keeping all of the balls in the air, Dave offers the following strategies for others who manage multiple priorities.

1. **Assign and delegate tasks before you respond.**
   If you begin your day by reading new mail, delegate what you can before you respond. You may find that others can handle the tasks better, or provide you with useful information to help you respond. Where appropriate, ask the person to whom you delegate the message to respond directly to the original sender, with a cc to you. This saves time and keeps you from being an E-mail bottleneck. Most people just want an answer and they don't care where it comes from.

2. **Plan your day.**
   The remaining tasks have to be done by you, but is today the best day, or should they be scheduled for another time? If you have an integrated contact manager, such as Microsoft Outlook, you can prioritize and schedule your tasks all in one place. If not, enter your tasks in your calendar, daybook or personal information manager.

3. **Reply to messages in the afternoon.**
   Once you have collected the necessary details, and received answers from those you have delegated the tasks to, you are ready to respond. Your goal is to reply to everyone who E-mailed you that day by closing time, or at least before the next morning, when they will sort through their E-mail.

Mark your messages with the proper priority

Not all messages are equally urgent or import. Messages from customers and your boss are always important and may be urgent. Read those messages before the rest of your in-box. Many E-mail systems allow you to mark an urgency level on the messages you send. Encourage your staff and colleagues to use this feature appropriately. Everyone needs to understand that the value of sending a message marked "high priority" is lost when all messages are set to that level.

If your E-mail system does not provide a priority feature, write a subject line that will help the recipient classify the message. One convention is to use two exclamation marks (!!) to begin the subject of an urgent message.

Sort your messages

Resist the temptation to read all of your messages. Information messages from list servers and other sources may be important but are seldom urgent. They can be stored for later reading or for reference. Where there are several messages with a common thread, read the latest first. You may not need to read the earlier messages at all. If you receive jokes from others, move them to a folder where you can return to read them later, perhaps on your lunch hour. (If you are overwhelmed by the volume of mail in your in-box, you might choose to politely ask the joke-senders to take you off their circulation lists.)

```
TO: Roy
FROM: Wayne

Hi Roy

I wish I had more time to read the jokes
you have shared with me but my in-box is
overflowing. Before I lose control of my
in-box, I am forcing myself to cut back.
Could you please remove me from your list?

Thanks

Wayne
```

Create folders on your computer for each project you work on. Move all correspondence into the appropriate folders. When the project is over, you can either delete the entire folder or archive it–perhaps on a floppy disk.

TIP: If your E-mail application has a "sent mail" folder you will need to delete items out of this folder from time to time. If a particular response is part of a project, move the message to the appropriate project folder. This way you will have both sides of the conversation on file for future reference.

Set a time limit

If E-mail is not a business-critical application for you, don't let it distract you from your work. Determine what times of the day are your most productive and make this an E-mail blackout period. If you typically run out of steam at 3:00 in the afternoon, schedule half an hour or so then to review your messages. Stick to the time limit you have chosen. Don't let E-mail distract you and eat up your day. Without time limits, I could spend an entire day sorting and reading the in-box on my desk. By quickly sorting discretionary mail into one pile, I can simply throw it away if I run out of time. My E-mail system is no different.

TIP: Some companies now discourage the use of E-mail during certain hours in an effort to get employees talking again!

If you have been out of the office for a while...

Scan your messages and read the newest ones first. If you see more than one message from an individual, chances are the most recent contains more information, or tells you that they have already received the answer they need.

Set up filters

If you subscribe to mailing lists, it is important that your E-mail client provide you with a way to automatically sort messages and store them in specific folders. Eudora is an excellent Internet mail client for this. Many corporate E-mail systems, such as GroupWise from Novell or Exchange from Microsoft, include these features. Microsoft Outlook 98 also provides this capability to Internet mail users.

You can set up your rule to recognize the subject of the message and automatically file information-only items away. You might never look at these items but they are filed for future reference if you ever need them.

> **TIP:** If you have an automatic rule that sorts messages based on the subject, be aware that if the subject line is not exactly the same for each message, your rule will not work.

Set aside the cc'd items you receive

Do you regularly read the messages that people copy to you for your reference? If your in-box is jam-packed with cc'd items that you can't seem to get around to, you may miss some of the important messages sent directly to you.

Set up an E-mail rule that automatically moves all carbon copy items to one folder so you can refer to them later if you wish. Establish a reasonable time limit by which you will delete these messages.

Keep copies of standard messages you send

If you have to respond to the same question repeatedly, why not save the response and re-use it the next time you need to answer that question again? Better yet, post the response in a public area such as your Web site. You can build a list of Frequently Asked Questions (FAQ) where others can find their answers.

If your E-mail system does not let you save messages, compose a document using your word processor. This way you can spell-check your message as well. In order to send the message, copy the text from the document and paste it into your new E-mail message.

> **TIP:** If you are a Windows user, CTRL+C copies highlighted text and CTRL+V pastes it in your current application.

Save time with autorespond

If you are frequently asked for the same information, such as sales literature, set up a rule to autorespond so that you don't have to. I knew one employee who joked that his rule autoresponded to any message his boss sent him with the response "GREAT IDEA," and then it deleted the message. ☺

Set up a three-step filing system

Many E-mail clients allow you to create folders and sub-folders to store information. (Your E-mail system administrator might disable this feature to encourage you to delete messages more frequently.)

Create folders for your projects and also for your information items. Set up a rule to automatically move material—newsletters, for example— to appropriate folders. Begin by moving new messages to a subfolder titled "New." At the end of each week (or month), move unread items from New to a subfolder called "Recent," and move Recent to a third folder called "Remove." If you decide that any information more than three months old can be discarded, then every three months delete the entire contents of the Remove folder without reading a single message.

WARNING: If you do start to read the contents of the Remove folder, you will have second thoughts and this will ruin everything. ☺

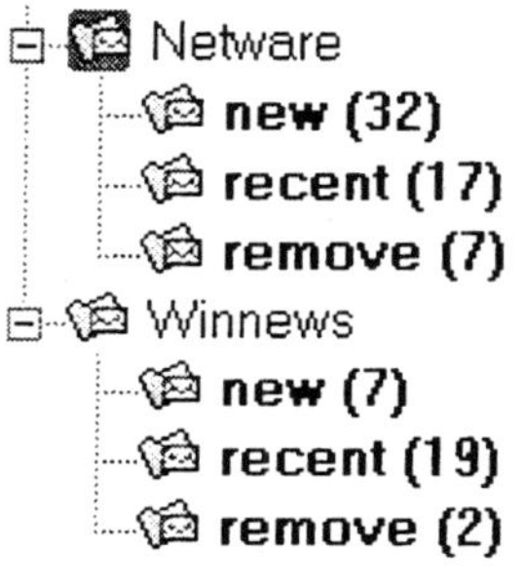

Once this folder is empty, move the contents of the Recent folder to the Remove folder, and move the new items to the Recent folder. Any time during the week you can read the contents of any of these folders, keeping in mind that at the end of the cycle you must throw away the contents of the Remove folder without looking at them.

NOTE: You will notice that Microsoft Outlook indicates the number of unread messages in each mailbox. This is useful if mail is routed automatically, because you can quickly see that you have new mail.

Create an archive folder and date it

Any information that you just can't bring yourself to throw out should go to your "Archive" folder. Make the title of that folder today's date. Make a promise to yourself that if it is still there at this time next year you will throw it out without even looking inside. Remember, you will sabotage your plan if you do so much as peek at its contents.

When sorting and filing, your biggest enemy is your curiosity and interest. I have gone missing for hours on trips to my basement to clean up or to look for something. If I so much as peek inside a box containing a collection of old magazines I may never be seen again.

Make decisions based on the message header (subject line)

If you have trained your contacts to use descriptive subject lines on their messages, you should quickly be able to make filing or action decisions based on the subject. This is even more important when you are traveling, since many E-mail applications allow you to view the headers even before downloading the messages.

Use previews to sort and delete (resist the temptation to read)

If you're swamped with E-mail, quickly scan your messages. If the subject line does not provide enough detail, the preview function provided by many E-mail programs allows you to see the first few lines of text without opening the message.

Practice what you preach. Write informative subject lines. If your message requests action, mention that right at the top, so your reader doesn't have to wade through the message to prioritize it.

If everyone you communicate with uses this rule, you will not need to read a message past the header if you can see it is not critical information. File it appropriately.

You can't read them all!

If you receive only a few E-mail messages a day, this is likely not a problem for you. But if you are swamped, it is useless to try to keep up. Be selective about which information items you read. Remove yourself from mailing lists that you never get around to reading. If you are fortunate enough to have an assistant, prepare a list of criteria that he or she can use to evaluate whether or not you need to personally respond to each message.

Don't jeopardize your family time, your income or your sanity by becoming a full-time message handler and personal advisor to the world. Lawyers are masters at reserving their time for paying customers. Who are your paying customers? Some people will take everything you give them and still ask for more. By answering their questions, you invite them to ask again. If you find that your good-natured willingness to help is being taken advantage of, refer the offender to a book or other resource, with a kindly worded message such as:

```
"I would like to help you further, but my
other commitments do not leave me enough time.
You should be able to find answers to your
questions in the book titled XXX.
```

An alternate approach is to make your response very brief. In trying to be polite, we often send out the message that we would be happy to continue helping. This example shows a polite but conclusive response to a request for help:

```
Question: Hi! Could you tell me how to XXX?
Answer: Please refer to page 10 of your user's
manual.
```

What your organization can do

In your organization, how much valuable information goes unnoticed, or is found only after it is needed?

Here are some tips you can use to help reduce the information overload many employees face. Remember, information is only valuable when the recipient is interested in it!

1. There is no need to share absolutely every thought or idea you have. Only the important ones, and only with those who are truly interested.
2. Identify the subject matter experts in your organization. Direct all relevant correspondence their way, and make sure everyone else is aware of who the keeper of the information is.
3. Save up bits of information to share at the next meeting or conference call rather than providing it in a continuous stream of trivial items.

Chapter 3-2

Avoiding Addiction and Burnout

These Techies even check their E-mail when they get up at night to take a wiz!
An Executive Observation

This chapter is for the overwhelmed and the E-mail addicts—the people who receive dozens or even hundreds of E-mail messages per day, or the ones who wish they did.

One of the big problems of E-mail communications is that E-mail can be addictive. For example, it is gratifying to receive thanks for a job well done or for information you forward to someone else. For the author, writing a book is a roller coaster full of ups and downs. While writing this book I hung on to many E-mail messages from those who sent me positive feedback. Whenever I started to doubt the value of the book, I read their comments and got all fired up again.

For people working at home, E-mail may be one of their only contacts with the outside world. For their corporate counterparts, it can be an escape from the office while still at one's desk.

These little gratifications throughout the day can be addictive. Like a kid waiting for a letter from a pen pal, you anxiously await a new E-mail message... from anyone!

In a corporate network you are always connected. If you are automatically notified when a new message arrives, you may not waste much time checking for mail (although you may waste a great deal of time reading frivolous messages).

When you are not connected to a network, you can waste a lot of time dialing in to check your mail. You know it disrupts your train of thought, but you convince yourself that the wait for your computer to make the modem connection really doesn't take long. You sacrifice those precious moments to get your E-mail fix.

I realize that many people need to check in regularly for messages so that they can reply in a timely fashion, but for the true E-mail addicts, popping out to the Internet just one more time to check the mail is no different than popping just one more quarter in a slot machine or video game.

For all those who wait with anticipation for one more E-mail message, there are others who dread the flood of messages they see every time they open their in-box. The anxiety can be overwhelming: "How can I possibly get to the bottom of this list?"

If you do not fit either of these profiles, feel free to skip this chapter. But if you need to stop being a slave to E-mail, I offer the following suggestions.

Pick up the telephone or meet with someone

If you are starving for attention or gratification, sometimes it is best just to give in. Pick up the telephone and get an entire conversation over with in minutes instead of dragging it out over days. Once satisfied, move on and get some work done so you can have fun tonight.

Take an "E-mail vacation"

Many tasks require a great deal of concentration. When you are in a state of "flow," you can accomplish a piece of work quickly. Like a salmon swimming upstream, you will reach your day's goal if you are focused, but if you are interrupted you can slide back and not make any progress at all.

One of the things I find effective is to turn my telephone ringer off while I'm working on a project. By scheduling uninterrupted time I get more accomplished. Sometimes I will even pick up my notes and walk to some other part of the building where people can't find me.

Recently my friend Arnold took a week's vacation from E-mail in order to complete a project. By the time he began checking messages, many of them no longer mattered because people had found their answers elsewhere.

As a courtesy to your correspondents, see in Chapter 6-2 of this book how to hang out your "gone fishing" sign while on your vacation from E-mail.

Turn off your E-mail notifier

E-mail is supposed to be unobtrusive, so why do you let it interrupt you when you are busy? If your E-mail system automatically notifies you of each incoming message, turn that feature off when you don't want to be distracted.

Schedule a time to check your E-mail

Plan your day in constructive blocks of time dictated by the type of tasks you have for that day or week. Allow yourself to check your E-mail only after you have completed a task. Even the biggest projects can be broken down into smaller chunks that will give you a sense of accomplishment.

Keep busy!

Being distracted by things you enjoy is natural. We usually allow it to happen when we are procrastinating on other tasks that we do not enjoy. Dive in to your projects and keep busy. Once you are on a roll, time will fly by and you will be less distracted by the need to check for mail. If you have a hard time starting a project, get a partner to help you outline your work or to brainstorm. Just like when going to the gym to work out, you are much more likely to stick to it if you have a partner. Use the buddy system when you hit a roadblock. We are less likely to slack off when we have someone else who is dedicated to the task working with us.

Do not check E-mail at the end of the day

Some people find that checking their E-mail is a good way to wind down before leaving the office. Others find it a terrific way to raise their stress level.

If you find that work has taken over your life, begin to take your life back by making more time for yourself.

Most people's days consist a series of successes. As they complete one thing and move on to the next, they feel a sense of accomplishment. However, the accomplishments of the day can be negated by starting a new task that cannot be completed before the end of the day.

In his book *Breathing Space: Living and Working at a Comfortable Pace in a Sped-Up Society*, Jeff Davidson writes that by taking on a new task that you cannot complete by the end of the day, you can set yourself up for frustration. If you have accomplished a lot today, wind up your day on a successful note— don't start something you can't finish, or you may go home feeling that you haven't accomplished anything.

If you have a habit of looking at your E-mail in the evening, make a point of ignoring it at least a few days a week, or make a change: decide to look at it only during working hours. Rather than thinking about work, cut yourself loose and enjoy some down-time away from E-mail and any other form of communication with the office.

Move! Change your address!

The time-wasting correspondents in your life may not go to the effort of locating you again. Be sure to notify your truly important contacts, and remember to change the E-mail address on your business cards and letterhead.

Make frequent referrals

Don't try to be all things to all people. Just because you *can* do something doesn't mean you should. Determine what your specialties in life and work really are. If questions come to you that are outside of your self-determined scope, be honest with yourself and with your contacts. Let them know. As you build your network of contacts, you will be able to advise people where they can go for answers. This strategy has a double benefit:

1. You will drastically cut down on distractions and wasted time.

2. You will build a trust with your network of contacts.

The people you refer others to will appreciate the business, and might return the favor when someone requires your expertise. The people you refer will appreciate your honesty and integrity. When they need your particular services they'll likely bring you their business.

Do something drastic—delete your in-box!

If you are still completely overwhelmed, delete all of your messages and start over.

If you need information from someone later, don't be ashamed to ask for it— everyone misplaces things sometimes.

DISCLAIMER: Empty your in-box only to preserve your sanity. This technique may not be appropriate for some job situations, and regularly deleting all your messages may be detrimental to your career.

What to do when you receive a message:

- Respond with a standard reply stating that you have received the message and it will be X days before you will have a chance to reply in detail, accepting or rejecting the task.
- Can you forward it to someone else? (Be sure to keep the sender in the loop.)
- File messages by project, and set up a reminder for yourself.
- Schedule time to respond.
- Keep your in-box organized and clean. (*This is habit-forming.*)

Chapter 3-3

Escaping from Spam and Junk Mail

"Spamming is the scourge of electronic mail and newsgroups on the Internet. It can seriously interfere with the operation of public services, to say nothing of the effect it may have on any individual's E-mail system... Spammers are, in effect, taking resources away from users and service suppliers without compensation and without authorization."

—Vint Cerf, Senior Vice-President, MCI Communications Corporation and acknowledged father of the Internet

Spam is a term used to describe junk E-mail. The worst type comes from unscrupulous scam artists who believe that if they send out enough junk mail, a worthwhile number of people will buy their product or fall for their scam. The typical spammer is usually a vendor who either doesn't realize the burden he or she puts on recipients, or don't care.

Spam is notorious because in many cases the recipient pays for receiving mail. And a number of companies have seen their entire E-mail systems brought down by a load of spam. Pacific Bell, for example, lost service for several days in March 1998.

The worst spammers use your Internet Service Provider's E-mail server to send mail to thousands of other recipients. Therefore, many service providers now prevent anyone from sending using their server if they are connected via another service provider. See Part 6 of this book, "Tips for the Traveler," about how to legitimately use E-mail on the road in spite of this.

The following is an excerpt from an ad for a spamming tool. I have included it to emphasize the point that true spammers will do anything to hit as many mailboxes as possible.

> This unique, first-of-its-kind software allows you to easily send 250,000 E-mail messages an hour, simply by making a single connection to the Internet using a standard modem, and connecting to either 20 different mail servers or a single mail server 20 times.
>
> -Personalize your E-mail messages with "Dear *recipient's address.*" This will increase positive responses dramatically.
>
> -Send E-mail messages 20 times faster than ever before.
>
> -Randomizes your user name or domain name during mailing. Works great if you have a domain name with unlimited aliases.

For more information on spam, and how to avoid being classified as a spammer, see Part 4 of this book, "Use E-mail as a Marketing Tool." For ways to eliminate spam, read on.

Keep a separate E-mail address for your on-line postings

One of the best ways to stop receiving junk mail is to move! After I moved to my new house a few years ago, it took months for the junk mail to start arriving again, and when it did there was not as much as before. If you have had the same E-mail address for some time, you may be receiving more nuisance mail than you would like. (Remember that if you change your E-mail address, the people you want to communicate with you may not be able to find you.)

Before the junk mail piles up, get a second E-mail address. You can use your "public" address for posting messages on the Internet and publish it on your Web site (if you have one), and give your private address only to people you know. From time to time, you can change your public address to escape all of those marketing lists that you have been added to.

Post your address using a non-standard format

Marketing companies that are notorious for spamming cruise on-line areas of the Internet to collect E-mail addresses. Sophisticated "robots" search for texts that looks like E-mail addresses. Prevent your address from being picked by making it invisible to these robots. One way is to change the format. For example, info@ITcoach.com can instead be written as info(at)ITcoach.com.

This format looks enough like a typical Internet E-mail address for most people to understand, but the robots will likely miss it. The downside is that if someone does want to contact you they cannot simply click on your E-mail address. Instead, they will have to compose a message manually and enter your proper address.

Another way to evade the robots is to plant a phony word, such as "junkmail," in your address. For example, I might post my return address as *wayne@junkmail.ITcoach.com*. In my message, I must instruct recipients to remove the "junkmail" from my return address in order to respond to me. I am not as big a fan of this method because it can be confusing; it is not obvious that my actual address is *wayne@ITcoach.com.*

Don't respond to unsolicited E-mail, even to ask to be removed from the list

In the movie *Jurassic Park*, the victims hid from the mighty Tyrannosaurus Rex by remaining still. The victims avoided detection until someone panicked and ran screaming into the night.

By responding to an unsolicited E-mail message, you let the sender know where you are and that your address is valid. Ignore the message altogether and you can go about your business undetected. They suspected that you were there, but if you are lucky they will give up and remove you from their list, thinking that they had an invalid address.

Many spammers rent address lists. The owner of the list charges a fee for a one-time use and often plants a few trick addresses to detect if the list is used more than once. Respond to a spammer's E-mail message and you have just added yourself to the spammer's own list. They no longer need to rent your name from someone else.

Set up a spam filter on your E-mail software

E-mail client software has become more sophisticated and feature-rich. By setting up specific rules, your E-mail program can automatically sort, respond to and delete messages. If you receive junk mail from a particular address, set up a filter that will automatically file or delete any message they send to you.

Examples of what filters can do for you:

- Maintain a list of your top-priority contacts, and move everything else out of your in-box.
- Filter out unwelcome known addresses.
- Filter based on message text. Look for common phrases such as "Dear xxx," or "This E-mail is never sent unsolicited..."

Find what works for you depending on the types of messages you receive.

Tell your service provider to block all traffic from offending senders

Your Internet Service Provider (ISP) likes spam even less than you do. If you experience problems with a spammer, notify your ISP. They may ask for a copy of the message and investigate. If they determine that the sender is breaking their rules on spamming, they can block all incoming traffic from that location. This will also help your fellow ISP subscribers. Unfortunately, spammers frequently change their addresses so this may not work for long.

Recently, my Internet Service Provider implemented a commercial spam filter to weed out junk mail from the newsgroups that they support. They reported filtering out over 500,000 messages in five days!

Delete spam and get on with your life

One commercial spammer, who provided a service to product companies that wanted to use the Internet to advertise, included a 1-800 number for recipients to call to order products. This backfired when, in an act of retaliation, everyone that got spammed called the toll free number to waste valuable long-distance minutes at the spammer's expense!

Retaliation worked that time, but don't try to get revenge against spammers. They may retaliate against you. Using an automated process, they are capable of adding your name to every mailing list on the Internet, bombarding you with so many messages that you will be unable to use your E-mail account.

My advice? Just delete the message and get on with your life.

IV

Part IV

E-mail Marketing Without Mistakes

Chapter 4-1

What You Need to Know Before You Begin

Introduction to the Issues

"Legitimate businesses are afraid to use E-mail to communicate with their customers because they're afraid of being branded spammers."

"Consumers are afraid to give out their E-mail address because they're worried about being added to mailing lists."

- David Kramer, attorney at Wilson Sonsini Goodrich & Rosati

Objective: Avoid alienating customers and generating negative publicity

One of the most heated topics of dispute between the business community and the Internet users from academic and research environments is the commercialization of the Internet. Tops on the list of Internet taboos is the practice of spamming or mass mailings.

By definition, spamming is the indiscriminate broadcasting of mail messages generally intended as advertising, but in a practical sense, an individual will feel spammed if they receive repeated unsolicited E-mail of any type. You see, the real definition is that spam is junk mail, a nuisance and unwanted.

The Internet community has begun a fight against spam for a number of reasons, not the least of which is the fact that it is a big nuisance. According to George Vrandenburg, Senior Vice-President at America Online (AOL), *spam can make up as much as 30 percent of the network traffic generated on AOL each day.*

The problem goes even further than using up available network bandwidth and server capacity. Angry customers can place a heavy load on their Internet Service Provider's support staff by lodging complaints about being spammed.

Another factor that is often overlooked is that not everyone receives E-mail free. Many companies outsource their E-mail services to other companies such as AT&T or ACEMail. Each provider has their own method of charging for the service, whether it is based on connect time, number or volume of messages received or perhaps a flat fee, so it is very possible that the recipient of your message is paying to receive it.

I had an experience a few years ago when I used my CompuServe mailbox to receive Internet mail. CompuServe mail was a free part of my CompuServe account as long as the messages were to and from other CompuServe mail accounts. A service charge was added to any Internet message, and one month these service charges added up to $56.00 just for junk mail!

A training company in California had sent a mass mailing to a list using something called a list server that processes each message. The problem was that the server's list was "open," meaning that any recipient could respond to the list, and the response would be sent to all other recipients on the list. Over the course of a few days, I received hundreds of messages from this list server as people either wanted to attend the advertised seminar, or wanted to be removed from the list. Like me, many people sent angry responses questioning why others were telling them their problems. Eventually, after about a month the flow of messages subsided but the lingering resentment towards this company has stuck in the minds of many who experienced the frustration of being inundated with unwanted messages that they couldn't stop, and being charged to receive them.

Spam or junk mail is not limited to the Internet. Many corporate users, unaware of the impact of their actions, send out non-commercial advertising all the time. Looking for people to join your company softball team? Celebrating a retirement?

Recruiting volunteers? If you use E-mail to distribute this type of information you may be just as guilty of overflowing mailboxes and taxing the system as your neighbor who is trying to sell that lovely AMC Pacer automobile.

The Impact of Spam

- Users receive more mail than they can deal with—wastes time and clouds important information.
- Users may be charged to receive the information.
- Computer networks jam up with unwanted E-mail.
- E-mail servers fill to capacity, or slow down as a result of overload.
- Service providers experience increased overhead that may be passed on to the consumer.
- People stop relying on E-mail as an effective means of communication.

Who are these spammers?

In my opinion, there are two types of spammers on the Internet. The first type may be ignorant to the rules of Internet etiquette, or "netiquet," as it has come to be known. If you are used to sending product literature out to your target market, this new medium is another vehicle for conducting business—but LEARN THE RULES!

The second type of spammer is in the business of distributing information on behalf of others. This is like the company that sends you packets of product cards, and pay to have their business literature included in the package.

The real problem lies with the latter commercial spammer since they frequently send advertisements to any E-mail address they can collect. They will distribute anyone's product information for a fee. They may also rent out their lists.

Many businesses believe that having access to such a large number of recipients will guarantee enough favorable results to offset any negative publicity their spam generates.

Unfortunately, many businesses are not aware that this practice is not condoned on the Internet, and they may subscribe to a spammer service with good intentions. And other advertisers just don't care.

While I don't condone the practice of broadcasting E-mail messages indiscriminately, I do believe that E-mail can be a very effective method of distributing information to interested recipients. If you provide products or services, you may already have a list of loyal customers who look forward to receiving your latest information.

If you are interested in finding out more about why spam has become such a problem, you can read the Frequently Asked Questions at http://spam.abuse.net/faq.html on the Internet.

Chapter 4-2

Rules For Creating a User-Friendly Marketing Program

"E-mail is like dynamite. In small, well-placed bursts it can be very powerful and helpful, but used the wrong way it can do irreparable damage."

- Michael J. Hughes, Personal Management Skills Coach

Establish your own code of ethics to avoid becoming an E-mail spammer

Only you can decide if you will be a friend or foe to E-mail recipients. Whatever action you take, you will have to live with the results. I recommend that each individual decide what their own personal code of ethics will be before beginning to use an E-mail system.

It's like deciding how you will behave when driving your car. My personal rule of the road is that my actions should not affect those around me. If I choose to drive faster than someone ahead of me, I should be patient and wait for a place to pass rather than tailgating, or, worse, risking both our lives in a frantic attempt to get by. If I drive more slowly than those behind me, I should move over to let them by, or if I pull out ahead of someone I should accelerate quickly so that they do not have to slow down to avoid me. I can quickly evaluate any move I make against one simple criterion: "Did I affect anyone else?" Not everyone has the same code of driving ethics. Some could evaluate their behavior by asking, "Have I run anyone off the road today?" Others take pride in how many people like me they can keep from speeding by driving slowly in the left lane.

When preparing to market with E-mail, you need to establish a criteria or code of ethics that you are comfortable with. All of your correspondence should carry the message that you are a quality person, worth doing business with. E-mail is but one more way to communicate your values and integrity.

Before you send that next message, ask yourself if you are adding value by sending someone information... or are you increasing their overload unnecessarily? The more you know about the recipient, the more accurate your decision will be. For instance, if I know that you are going through a stressful period while you try to finish a project, I may decide not to send information that will distract you. On the other hand, if you ask me for a solution to a business problem and I have a product or information that I think will help you, I will not hesitate to share this information with you.

Build and maintain lasting relationships

I am an active motorsports fan and participant. Whether by conscious decision or not, I tend to be loyal to companies that support my sport, and show my loyalty by purchasing their products.

Last summer I was at a store looking for a case of motor oil and I stopped to read the label of a brand I had not even considered buying before. But there I was making the decision to choose that product. The only explanation I have is that that at a motorsports event that year, I was attracted to a motorcycle on display that was sponsored by that company. That was the beginning of the relationship that the company has since established with me. They have continued by letting me know how their teams are doing in competition and the dates of races in my area, and providing a hospitality area at various events. My loyalty has grown far beyond any I ever had to their competitors, who I know comparatively little about.

Many organizations build strong relationships using regular newsletters. If these provide value, then why not cut the cost of distribution and use E-mail? If a formal newsletter is not your thing, then perhaps you can forward information, as you find it, that you know would interest the recipient.

The key is to ensure that the recipients consider your information valuable and want to receive it. Ideally, you should wait for them to ask for it, or at least start sending and then ask them if they want to continue receiving it. In either case, always give them a way of canceling, and tell them how in your message.

If you find the task of keeping track of all of your clients a daunting one, pick your best customers and serve them well. They may be the ones who buy the most products, or perhaps will pay a premium for your product since they buy in smaller quantities. Maybe your best customer is the prestigious one who will help you attract other clients.

Provide something of value in your message

One of the best ways to generate business is to become known as an expert, the one to call when someone needs a product you supply. And of the best ways to become known as an expert is to share your knowledge. ANYONE can benefit from taking this approach, even those who work for a large organization and don't think they have a product to sell. You are the product your manager hired, and those you work with rely on you for your skills. The more people that are aware of your skills, the more valuable you become.

Identify yourself as the keeper of the data that you specialize in. Advertise yourself as the magnet for the data that overflows their in-basket. If your "customers" can remove themselves from the stream of information that overwhelms them, they will be more relaxed and more effective. Most people collect far too much information for fear of not having enough when they need it. Your customers can relax, knowing that they have you as a resource when they need one.

If there is value in your list and you want to profit from it, come up with a technique that will add value for the recipients as well. Perhaps you could drop the price of a newsletter you now charge for in exchange for permission to include a brief advertisement with each issue. You might negotiate a product discount and pass it on to your recipients as a way of using your mailing list as an advertising medium. Electronic coupons can be added to your regular E-mailings to benefit you, your supplier and your customers. The bottom line is that the list is yours, and since you know your recipients so well, you can be the judge of what type of information is acceptable to send. Don't be afraid. You aren't spamming when you add value to your on-going communication.

If you have even a hint of doubt, survey your recipients beforehand. Make it short, quick and clear. Be sure they understand why you are asking the questions and what benefit they will derive from responding. "You will not be flooded with unwanted E-mail messages" is not a benefit to base their decision on. They shouldn't expect to be bombarded. Instead, say something like, "You will receive 30 percent off your next order," or include an offer for a free booklet or a product from one of your sponsors.

Keep information items short and to the point

It is far better to have someone call you looking for your service than for you to hound them with something they don't want. If you keep it short, they will come to you if they want more. For more information check out my monthly tip sheet at http://www.ITcoach.com.

Did I mention to keep it short?

Ask permission before sending advertising to a person's E-mail address

One day at lunch, a friend complained that some "bozo" in his organization kept sending him and all of his colleagues information collected daily from an Internet newsgroup. No one wanted to read the clippings, but the sender thought they did. They would all have preferred to simply know that that individual was a reliable source if the need for such information arose.

This was a case of information being disseminated within an organization, but equally annoying is the person on the Internet sending an advertising newsletter to a list of people who do not wish to receive it. Left unchecked long enough, this practice will build resentment among the recipients. At the very least, senders, always give them a way out. Let them know in each message that you will gladly remove them from the list if they so wish. Even better, ask them to subscribe before you begin sending them information.

Create a reason for people to seek your advice

So how do you get people to subscribe without sending them something first? Why not try going to them with a sample? I have mentioned to my wife that she should become a distributor for automatic bread maker machines. I bought her one for Christmas one year, and since then she has given away countless loaves of bread to friends and neighbors who have gone on to buy bread-makers of their own.

It began with a loaf for a neighbor who had dropped in for tea. Next, it was a kind gesture for a mother returning from the hospital with her newborn. Other people on the street began asking her about her bread maker and every request was answered with a warm loaf of fresh bread. After tasting the sample, virtually everyone purchased a machine of their own. What began as a simple gesture of kindness has turned her into the bread making guru of the area. People seek her out when their bread doesn't rise. Sounds like an excellent opportunity for a newsletter. ☺

Don't abuse your privilege

If someone has decided to subscribe to your mailing list, be sure to treat them with the respect they deserve. Provide them with the information on a timely basis but be careful not to overdo it. A brief survey can help focus your material and make your mailings more effective, but don't overuse the survey technique. To generate a higher number of successful returns, make your survey multiple-choice and not too long.

Once you receive an inquiry, request for information, or returned survey, be sure to respond quickly and follow up. One of the main reasons that people do not follow up with others they are trying to get a job with, sell a product to, or ask advice of is that they do not want to be a nuisance. E-mail can help these cautious individuals. Because it is less obtrusive than a telephone call, people tend to be much more willing to persist in pursuing contacts.

Consider carefully before selling your E-mail distribution list

As a reader, you come to this topic from one of two directions. If you are a marketing novice then cross off selling your E-mail list as a source of revenue. If you are a seasoned professional, think twice before treating your E-mail list the same as a contact list that you may already rent to others.

Building a qualified and focused E-mail list that will respond to you requires that you earn the recipients' trust. Show your integrity by not betraying this trust. Though it may be tempting to sell or rent your E-mail list to others, the problem is that you have no control over what is sent to the list. If your valued customers found out that you were responsible for them receiving an avalanche of E-mail, I guarantee that they would not be happy.

People on your circulation list want to receive your message and you have worked hard to gain their trust. Don't throw it all away for a few bucks.

Include your contact information in your own correspondence

How many times in your life have you spoken to someone and then later wondered how you could get in touch with them? You may have met on vacation or at a convention or show. At the time you didn't think that you would need to contact them again, but later you realized that they had information that would help you or someone you know.

The more we know about one another, the more likely it is that we will find common interests

When you meet someone do you exchange business cards? Why not have an electronic one too? You can include a simple tag line, known as an electronic signature, at the bottom of your E-mail message. This will do two things for you:

1. If someone reads about you and your services and they want to find out more, they can now contact you.
2. You save time. When you meet people on line, your "signature" gives them information about you without them having to ask. (It may turn out that one of the people you converse with is a neighbor you haven't met yet. This happened to me once.)

Make sure that your signature is not overly long. People are beginning to get sensitive to blatant advertising but this really depends on how you use E-mail. If you are concerned, add a simple signature to an E-mail message when you contact someone for the first time. If you have a legitimate reason for contacting them you should not have a problem. As your relationship grows, you can start sharing a more substantial list of your products, or mention promotional events. You may also have different signatures for different types of clients, or different situations. For instance, I have one simple signature that I use almost everywhere. I tag on additional information when communicating with friends, or if I am promoting a special event. In the last ten years, I have never had a problem because of signatures I have used.

Finally, don't forget to include your Web site address if you have one. Be sure to type it fully since many E-mail applications support hot links. This means if you provide a Web address such as http://www.ITcoach.com, the recipient will be able to double-click on the address and go directly to your site.

How do I create my electronic signature?

Many E-mail programs support electronic signatures. You create the signature once and then have it automatically added to your outgoing messages. If your E-mail program does not provide this feature, you can keep the information in a file and copy and paste to avoid re-typing it each time. Include your name, any contact information you wish to share, and a tag line that describes what your business is about.

If you can't say in one or two sentences what you do, it's time to work harder to define your niche. (You can contact the Niche Doctor at http://www.falkenstein.com for help.)

WARNING: If you are concerned about receiving junk mail, keep your address to yourself or send it only when asked. (I suspect, though, that keeping yourself obscure could be detrimental to your businesses success.) An alternate solution is to include a secondary E-mail address rather than your primary one: for example, info@yourcompany.com.

As an example, here is one of my electronic signatures:

```
-----------------------------------------------

Wayne McKinnon
The Information Technology Coach

-Keynotes        Tel (613)762-4608
-Briefs          Fax (613)825-4895
-2nd Opinion     info@ITcoach.com

Visit http://www.ITcoach.com for tips and news.

------------------------------------------------
```

Chapter 4-3

Examples of Successful E-mail Marketing

This chapter shows how you can use E-mail to enhance your marketing efforts. You can promote your business by E-mail without sending junk mail. And you can adapt many of these techniques to raise your personal visibility within your company. Look at Part 5 of this book, "Solving it with Technology," to choose tools and products to help you speed some of your tasks, such as automatically replying to customer inquiries.

Use on-line services for marketing

A few years ago when I was learning how to attract sponsors for my motorsports passion, I read an interesting article posted on CompuServe. At the bottom of the article was the electronic signature of Charlie Hayes, a motorsports consultant with The Action Group. Over the months, I noticed that Charlie did an excellent job of providing answers to anyone who asked about sponsorship. He answered several of my questions, with no strings attached.

Discussion groups, CompuServe forums, chat rooms, mailing lists and newsgroups are channels people use to meet each other and discuss topics of interest. Someone posts a question and others respond. You can find archives of this type of information on the Internet. The most popular Internet newsgroup archive is at http://www.dejanews.com.

Just as you might network by attending association meetings, investment clubs or trade breakfasts, on-line chat areas are a great place to share your knowledge and expand your network. Some are part of a larger on-line system such as America Online (AOL) or CompuServe. Many Internet Web sites have their own chat areas that draw a focused group of people. Lately I have listened in on some interesting discussions by visiting the Web sites of magazines. Many have chat areas or Web-boards where readers discuss current topics.

I responded to a question posted on the message board at the Home Office Computing site some time ago. Today, if you use the Alta Vista search engine (http://www.altavista.digital.com/) to search for "working on retainer" you will probably still find the Web page containing my answer. Home Office Computing can be found at http://www.smalloffice.com/. I answered the question simply because I had recently been discussing the same issue with a colleague and I thought I had something to add. I continue to receive favorable responses from this one simple message, which included my E-mail address.

Network by joining a mailing list

While many different Internet tools provide forums for discussion, the one that integrates most closely with your E-mail system is the Internet mailing list. This allows one person to send a message to an entire group of people who have joined a list. Every message goes to all members of the list, and all replies do as well. A mailing list is a great way to keep everyone in the loop—all list members can follow the entire discussion.

I warn you to be very selective about which lists you join. I subscribed to one general-interest list and received over 300 messages per day. Mailing lists, unless they are small and focused, are not as effective networking tools as are Web-chat and newsgroups.

Which newsgroups can you join, and how can you use them to network?

You access newsgroups using the newsreader software that comes bundled with your Internet Web-browser software, such as Netscape or Internet Explorer. Newsgroup discussions tend to be more structured and easy to follow than are mailing lists, and many are moderated to avoid duplicate messages or inappropriate topics.

Your Internet Service Provider subscribes to a series of newsgroups and stores this information on their server. You can subscribe only to the newsgroups that your ISP redistributes.

The important thing to remember about any form of knowledge networking is that you want to go where your potential clients are. Before posting any replies, visit the site a few times to see how other people respond. You should also be very careful not to come across as a salesperson. People appreciate advice and the sharing of knowledge, but don't appreciate a salesperson flogging wares and cluttering up an information system with advertising. Provide something of value, and over time people will begin to seek out your advice.

Compose your message off-line

To make sure my spelling is correct, and to give myself more time to think about what I am saying, I compose my message with my word processor. Once I have reviewed the message and am happy with its contents, I run the spelling and grammar checkers. To post the message, I simply highlight the text, cut, and paste to the on-line system. (*With Microsoft Windows*, **hold** the **control key** and press **C** to **copy** [**<cntrl C>**]; to **paste** use **<cntrl V>**.)

Many times, I have found that my thoughts are worth preserving for later use. For example, you may want to save some of your posts to use as replies to E-mail.

Sample posting to a newsgroup

```
From: John Q. Public

Subject: Race Dates???

Does anyone know if there is a race being held
at Mosport near Toronto in August? My nephew
will be visiting for the month and is a big race
fan. I would love to get him to the track for
the weekend while he is here.
```

Reply From Wayne McKinnon

Hi John,

The Vintage Motorcycle Festival is on August 22-23, and the IMSA sports car race is on August 30-31 this year.

I will be racing at both events. If you would like access to the paddock area let me know and we can meet up. Look for the "Big Sponsor" racing team tent.

Hope this helps.

Wayne McKinnon
The Information Technology Coach

-Keynotes	Tel (613)762-4608
-Briefs	Fax (613)825-4895
-2nd Opinion	Info@ITcoach.com

Visit http://www.ITcoach.com for tips and news.

Reply From: John Q. Public

Thanks, Wayne. If you need two extra pairs of hands for the weekend we would love to help out.

John and I have common interests that led us both to this CompuServe forum. I share with John some information that helps him plan his summer. At the same time, this gives me an opportunity to gain some exposure for my sponsor, "Big Sponsor," as well as for myself and my business—without abusing the system by advertising. The key to success is to participate for the enjoyment of sharing information. The business exposure is an added bonus.

⇒ John gets the information he is looking for.

⇒ I get a valuable pair of volunteers to help at the events.

⇒ My sponsor gets added exposure because others will read this post.

⇒ My Web site attracts more attention.

⇒ John and his nephew experience a weekend together that they will always remember.

NetMind gets permission to distribute E-mail

We all complain about the amount of junk we receive from the postal service. Each letter and flyer takes another slice of our already busy day. But other advertisements are not nearly as inobtrusive. How many people subscribe to magazines or industry newsletters that contain advertising, or are sponsored in some way? We accept this as part of doing business. We realize that advertisers offset the cost of publishing in return for the exposure their products get, and, besides, we can easily skip the ads if they do not grab our attention.

The same technique is used by advertisers who place banners on Internet Web pages, but how do you apply this technique to E-mail? Let's quickly review some basic rules of sending E-mail:

⇒ People do not want to find over 100 advertisements in their mailbox each morning.

⇒ We know that people want only E-mail that provides some value.

⇒ It is okay to send advertisements by E-mail if we obtain the recipient's permission.

One quick note on this last point is that you must not abuse the privilege of sending advertisements to someone. You should not flood their mailbox just because they wanted to receive notification of your product updates and new releases.

NetMind has come up with an ingenious way of providing value to Web surfers, Webmasters/publishers and advertisers. They have created a win/win/win situation by providing a free service to people who want to be notified by E-mail when their favorite Web pages change. This insures that every message contains something of value, and since subscribers receive the message anyway, why not include an ad for one of the sponsors who made the service possible?

The NetMind Webmaster can also include a form from another Web page that users may be interested in subscribing to, such as my monthly tip sheet, found at http://www.ITcoach.com.

The advertiser benefits by being invited into peoples' mailboxes, co-marketing in the same way that a car rental company sends brochures along with your Airmiles statement. And to ensure that subscribers are not inundated with junk mail, NetMind promises not to release their mailing list to anyone.

This marketing system provides value to everyone:

⇒ **For the subscribers** - Timely notification of changes to their favorite Web pages.

⇒ **For the advertisers** - Promotional messages included in outgoing mail messages.

⇒ **For NetMind** - Revenue in exchange for providing a useful free service.

Here is a copy of the subscription form for NetMind (http://www.netmind.com):

Please enter your e-mail address and press the "Mind It!" button to receive e-mail from the free URL-minder service when the page at http://www.netmind.com/URL-minder/example.html changes.

MIND IT!

Your e-mail address will not be given to any third party and will be used only to deliver change-notices for the pages you request, and possibly, to inform you of changes in the status of the service, although such notices should be very infrequent. The service is ad-supported, and advertisements will appear in the change-notices themselves. Please read and agree to the terms and conditions below before signing up for this service.

Terms and Conditions:

This service is provided free of charge, on an "as-is" basis. Although NetMind applies its best efforts to maintain this service, no warranty is offered and no fitness for any particular purpose is guaranteed. By signing up for this service you agree that NetMind Services Inc. is not liable for any defects, lost profits, or any damages that may result from defects of any kind. You further agree that you are the owner of the e-mail address, which you are registering, or that you have the express permission of the owner to register that address with this service.

NetMind is against unsolicited e-mail (SPAM) as a matter of policy. You agree that as a sponsored service, messages sent to the above e-mail address in conjunction with this service may contain advertisements. You will not be sent any advertisement-only messages by NetMind. NetMind agrees not to knowingly divulge your e-mail address to third parties, and further that your e-mail address submitted here will only be used to provide and improve upon this service. You agree that NetMind is not liable for the acquisition of your address by third parties without NetMind's knowledge. You acknowledge that NetMind has no control over anything which occurs on servers not controlled by NetMind, including any forms for registering with this service which are not on NetMind's servers. NetMind agrees to take reasonable measures to protect your address and any other personal information submitted on NetMind's servers.

Free card shop advertises software company

Parsons Technology sells software products and games from their Web site. To increase traffic they provide a free greeting card service that allows people to create and send on-line greeting cards. Once the card has been created, it is saved in a private directory, and the address of that directory is E-mailed to the recipient. The E-mail message says that there is a greeting card waiting for them from the sender.

The E-mail message also contains contact information for Parsons Technology, along with a friendly request for input on ways to improve the service. When the recipient of the card visits the Web site to see their greeting, they will also read a note at the bottom of the page advertising the software product that was used to create the card. People I have spoken to that have tried the service find it a fun way to exchange greetings at special times of the year, such as Christmas or Valentine's Day, and they don't mind the commercial advertising that makes the service possible.

The greeting card shop is at
http://www.parsonstech.com/cstudio/CardShop/.

Urban legends: are they promotional tools?

I am not entirely convinced that some of the humorous stories or E-mail messages with funny typographical errors are accidents. I have nothing to base my suspicions on, but it seems that all of these stories involve some big company that would just love to stay fresh in the public's mind.

Humorous stories about misworded messages, or anecdotes passed on by customer support reps, spread like wildfire on the Internet. One example was the computer user who called XYZ company to ask if the coffee cup holder on his new PC was replaceable under warrantee. (It seems the CD-ROM carrier broke when the user mistook it for a coffee cup holder). People love to send these stories to their friends regardless of their validity, and I can't help but wonder if the company has released the story intentionally, to get publicity.☺

Be creative

Businesses that are shut out of common distribution methods must find creative methods to get visibility for their products. Tobacco manufacturers have successfully used motorsports to get television exposure when advertising on television is forbidden. They do this with banners at racetracks and signage on the cars. Are there similar methods that you could use for your products?

Part V

Technology Solutions to Your E-mail Problems

Chapter 5-1

Technology Primer

Behind every seemingly simple technology lies a series of complex systems. To place a telephone call there is no need to understand the underlying technology, but then telephone technology (telephony) has been around for some time. We have learned to adapt to it as much as we have learned to adapt it to us.

E-mail, on the other hand, is a relatively new way for society to communicate. Understanding how messages flow through the system can help you head off technical difficulties before they occur.

Throughout this book, I have focused on ways that you can adapt to the technology. In the next few sections I will also introduce a few helpful tools to assist you in ensuring that your message arrives.

Message systems

Only recently has Internet mail become a de facto standard for messaging systems. While Simple Message Transfer Protocol (SMTP) has been the standard for Internet mail for some time, other proprietary solutions have been predominant in the corporate world.

As companies' requirements for messaging solutions increased, companies such as Novell, Microsoft, Lotus and a slew of other manufacturers responded by offering products that could handle the transfer not only of text-based mail messages, but also attachments such as word processing files and spreadsheets.

Because the systems do not adhere to a "standard", manufacturers can add new features quickly, without waiting for the industry to approve each feature as part of a standard. By adding new features, each manufacturer hopes to gain a competitive advantage that will result in more product sales. But this proprietary mentality has made it difficult for systems from different manufacturers to co-exist and inter-operate.

To solve the inter-operability problem, E-mail gateways are used. The job of the gateway is to allow messages to flow between two dissimilar systems by translating the messages from one system into the format used by the other.

Unfortunately, gateways are not a perfect solution. If a component of a sent message is not supported by the receiving system, that component is lost. While the text of messages usually arrives intact, many times the attachments do not.

What happens to attachments?

The one common component to all E-mail systems is the message body. Every E-mail system is capable of transmitting a plain text message. But even this can be a problem.

Along with all of the message's other parts, the text has to appear in the correct location for the system to recognize that it is the message body.

To understand the problem, look at the example below. Each system has an order that it places message components in. When a message is transferred between systems that use different orders, as in the example below, the subject and message body from System 1 show up as attachments when sent to System 2.

Message System

Message System 1		Message System 2
TO:	⇒	TO:
FROM:	⇒	FROM:
CC	⇒	CC
BCC	⇒	SUBJECT
SUBJECT	⇒	ATTACHMENT1
MESSAGE BODY	⇒	ATTACHMENT2
ATTACHMENTS	⇒	MESSAGE BODY

Even if two systems can get the order of the message parts straight, there is still no guarantee that the attachments will make it. Internet mail is a simple system that was not designed to carry attachments. Consequently, developers have come up with many creative ways to combine an attachment with a message text.

An attachment is converted to standard text using a complex algorithm that looks at patterns within the attachment and assigns a text-string equivalent. *For example*, if I was to send a picture to you, the E-mail system I use might identify all blue dots with the combination <1Q>, and all white spaces with <1Y>. It would also specify their location.

When you receive the message, your E-mail system has to recognize my encoding scheme and convert the elements back to a picture. Otherwise, you end up with a string of meaningless text.

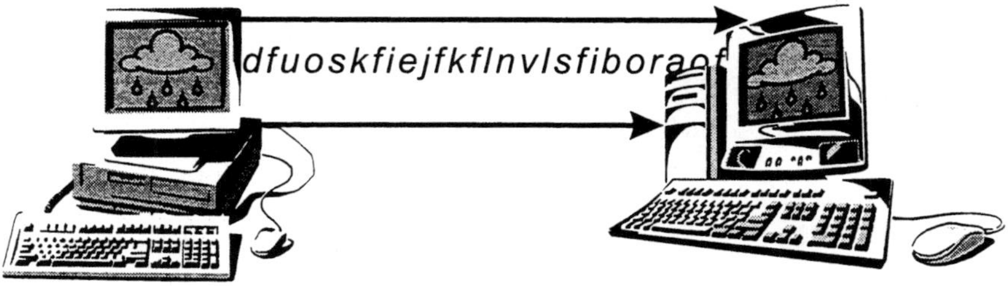

If the attachment to your mail message does not arrive intact, have the recipient call their service provider or network administrator to find out what encoding method is used at their end. Then find out if your system is compatible.

The SMTP Standard

Simple Message Transfer Protocol has become so widely recognized that virtually every commercial E-mail system can communicate using SMTP, either directly or through an SMTP gateway.

Today, many of the features that made proprietary messaging solutions so attractive are now available as part of the Internet suite of messaging products and standards that includes SMTP.

Since Internet mail standards are open to everyone, today the manufacturers of messaging systems comply with the Internet standards in order to inter-operate with messaging systems from other manufacturers. Messages can be transmitted from one person to another, or from one company to another, regardless of the messaging system used. But we are not fully to the point of complete compliance and inter-operability.

This means that you may still have problems sending messages between two separate E-mail systems.

Where does your mail message go?

When you send an E-mail message it goes to your E-mail server, where it sits until the recipient picks it up. If the recipient does not have an account on your E-mail server, the message is forwarded from one E-mail server to another. Once it arrives at the recipient's mail server, he or she can then connect and retrieve the message.

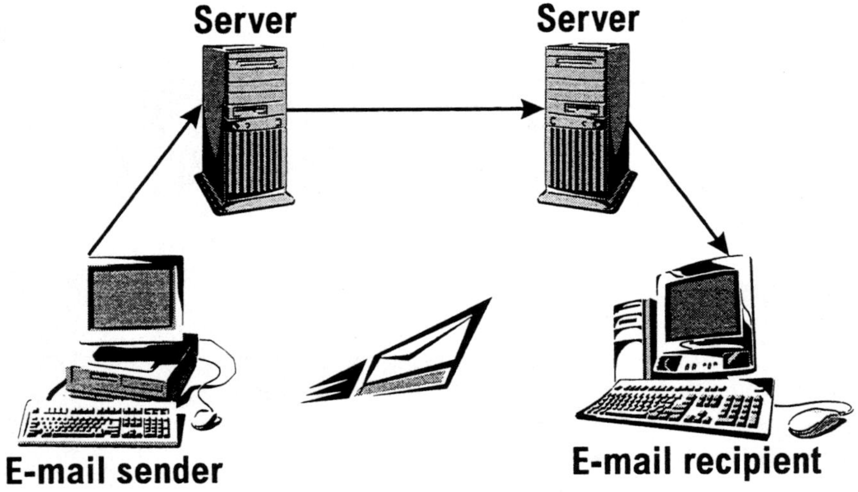

Depending on how your E-mail system is configured, once you retrieve your message it either moves to your local hard disk on your computer, or remains on the server. If it remains on the server, the advantage is that you can read the message from any location. If it is stored locally, you must use that computer to view the message.

Many people want to access their mail messages both from home and at work. If you have a portable computer, you carry your messages with you wherever you go. But if you have two computers, one at home and one at work, it may be best to leave the messages on the server so you can read them with either computer. Some E-mail client software allows the user to configure this option.

The Internet SMTP (Simple Message Transfer Protocol) mail does not let you keep already-read messages on the server to read again later. Instead, you must store them locally. One solution for travelers is to use a POP3 (Post Office Protocol) server and mail client that can be used to preview your messages. More recently, the IMAP4 (Internet Message Access Protocol) standard has been adopted to allow messages to remain on the server rather than requiring them to be stored locally.

Multiple E-mail accounts

Many people have just one E-mail account and use the same computer or E-mail client to retrieve messages. But you may have more than one message system—perhaps your business account on your corporate E-mail system, and your Internet mail account.

Many E-mail clients, such as Microsoft Outlook and Eudora Pro, allow you to connect to multiple mailboxes to retrieve messages. The advantage is that you need to look at the contents of only one in-box.

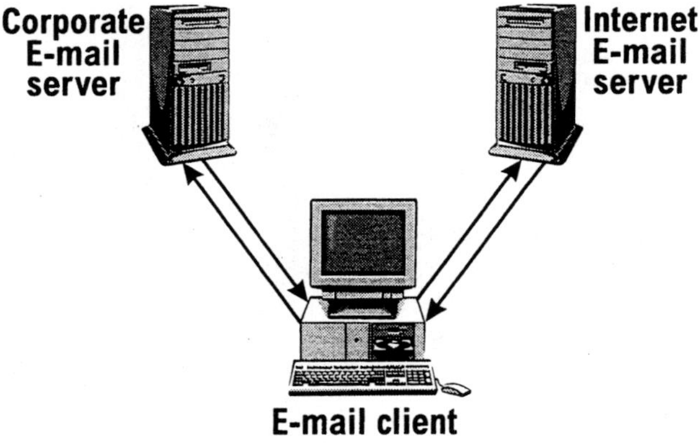

In other cases, you may have a reason to maintain multiple E-mail addresses but prefer to have all of your messages flow in to the same E-mail account. If you have Internet mail, your service provider creates an account for you. I recommend asking for at least one additional address or "alias" that directs mail to your one E-mail account. You could use this alias in any promotional material you distribute instead of providing your private address. An example is sales@yourdomain.com.

You may also create an alias to use when submitting your name to contests, on-line order forms, or any place that might get you on a mailing list. If the amount of junk mail sent to your alias gets out of hand, create a new one. Have your service provider delete the old alias and link the new alias to your E-mail account.

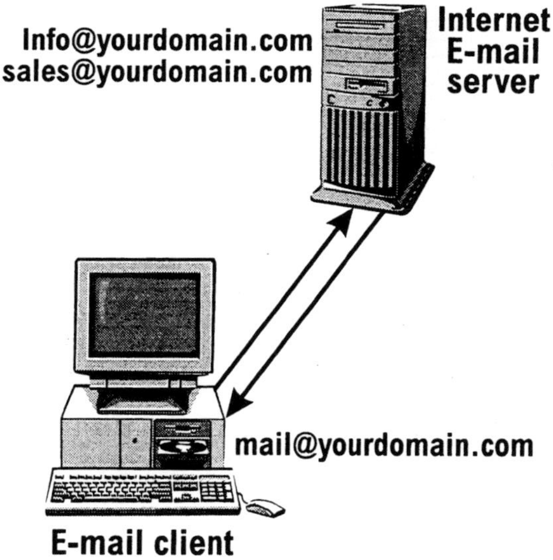

Virtual Domain

If you use Internet mail, you may want to create an easily recognizable E-mail address that promotes you or your Web site, or relates to what you do. The majority of Internet E-mail users have an address such as yourname@your.service.provider.com.

Your service provider can register a unique domain name for you and link your E-mail account to your new domain name. Why promote your service provider when you can promote your own company and make it easier for people to find you?

I am known as The Information Technology Coach™. I have registered an easy to remember domain name. (ITcoach.com). When I tell people my E-mail address, I am promoting my own domain, not my service providers. And, if you know my E-mail address Info@ITcoach.com, you can easily figure out my Web server address http://www.ITcoach.com.

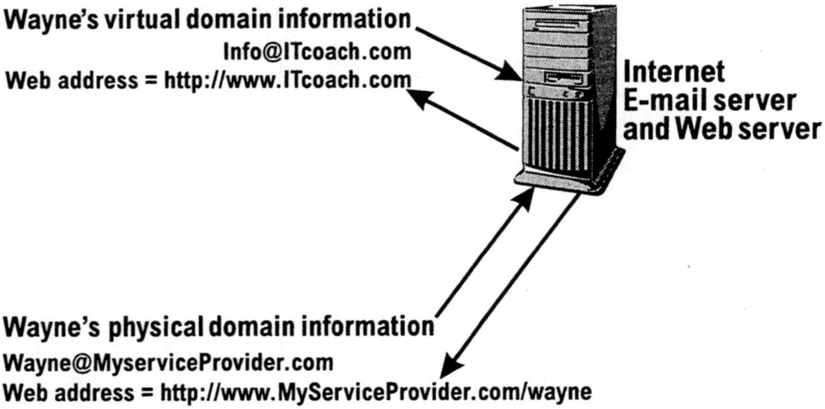

Chapter 5-2

Tools and Utilities

The intent of this book is to provide an-easy-to-read source of information that covers all of the bases without being too technical for the average reader. There are many great E-mail products on the market, and those products are always changing. To get a sense of the types of tools and utilities available, read on.

If you would like an up-to-date list of product names, visit my Web site at http://www.ITcoach.com/e-rules.

Do you know what happens when you send to multiple recipients?

When you send an E-mail message to multiple recipients using the "carbon copy" (cc feature), all recipients of the message can see the entire list of all other recipients.

If you run a business where confidentiality is important to your clients, how will they feel knowing that you have just announced to the world that they are one of your customers?

Worse yet, do you want your list to fall into the hands of a competitor?

The listserv solution

A list server is a computer that processes incoming messages and forwards them to a registered list of recipients. Lists can be "open," meaning that anyone can add themselves to the list by sending a registration-request E-mail message, or the list can be "closed," available only to pre-registered recipients.

If a discussion topic is of interest to many people, a listserv is an effective way of keeping everyone in the loop. One person's comments are forwarded to the entire list.

But listservs can also be used to distribute information from one person to many. A moderated list prevents other people's messages from being forwarded to the list. The moderator decides what should be sent and what should not.

A closed moderated list can be used to process an outgoing announcement to each recipient. Instead of sending one message to many, the one message is sent to each recipient individually, one by one.

If you want to automatically respond to messages or distribute information upon request, listservs and E-mail robots (programs that automatically read mail and respond, to deal with repetitive matters such as requests for product information) are the answer. Below is a list of some of the more popular listserv software:

SVList (*run from your desktop PC*)

http://www.cadvision.com/softventures

Imail	http://www.ipswitch.com/
ListCaster	http://www.mustang.com/
LetterRip	http://www.fogcity.com/
LIST	http://www.starnine.com/

Personal assistants

Personal assistants are E-mail clients that include an E-mail rule feature. Rules can be set up to automatically sort, filter, delete or respond to incoming messages. Some will even allow you to schedule your responses to be delivered at a certain time.

On the Internet, Eudora Pro is the most well-known full-featured E-mail client, but Microsoft Outlook 98 is also very powerful. In the corporate arena, Beyond Mail, Microsoft Exchange, Novell GroupWise and Lotus Notes all have some sort of E-mail rules capability.

There are two main challenges with E-mail rules:

1. If rules are client-based, the E-mail client must remain turned on and connected in order to automatically respond to messages.
2. If rules are server-based, users can overload a server's CPU resources by creating too many rules.

Fax gateways

Whether you are connected to a corporate E-mail system or are a stand-alone Internet mail user, there are many fax solutions designed to plug in to your existing system. The best solutions integrate closely with your E-mail client. They let you maintain one list of recipients and specify either an E-mail address or fax address for them. This is particularly useful for distributing material such as newsletters because you can reach both types of recipients in one easy step.

A corporate fax gateway solution allows you to send E-mail to a person who does not have an E-mail address. The message is instead forwarded to a fax server where is it converted to fax format and sent to the recipient's fax machine.

Honey, I shrunk the files!

There are many excellent products on the market that allow you to compress a file before attaching it to an E-mail message. WinZip (http://www.winzip.com) is my personal favorite. WinZip will not only compress a file, it will also uncompress and decode files of many formats regardless of what tool was used to compress the file.

WinZip works by creating an archive file. One or more files can be added to the archive and then zipped up or shrunk so that the file/s will fit on a floppy disk, or take up less space and transmit faster over E-mail systems.

It truly is a one-stop tool for dealing with incoming or outgoing file attachments.

How E-mail security works

If you are concerned about the contents of your E-mail message falling into the wrong hands, you can encrypt the message before sending. Encryption is a process used to convert a message into an unreadable and therefore secure format. When the message is received by an authorized recipient, it is un-encrypted so they can read it.

Encryption utilities scramble the contents of the message using a complex encryption algorithm. The only one who can decode the message is someone who holds the key to unlocking the file (knowing the decryption algorithm necessary to convert the file back to a readable form).

There are different encryption methods, all based on the number of "bits" used to encrypt the message. Think of the number of computer bits as being similar to the numbers on a combination lock you might use to secure your bicycle or gym locker.
The longer the combination is, the more difficult it is to crack.

Due to law enforcement concerns, the governments of various countries may require a method of unlocking secure data. Concerns range from tracking illegal activities to plotting to overthrow the government. The Wassenaar Arrangement is a 33-nation agreement that requires export controls on encryption software, lest an uncrackable technology fall into the hands of enemies. Currently, countries can export software that uses 40-bit encryption, but 128-bit is regarded as necessary for truly secure electronic commerce.

The general belief among exporting countries is that the government must be provided with a means of unlocking secure documents. Companies producing the software are required to deposit a master key with the government to satisfy this requirement.

New encryption schemes include S/MIME (Secure Multipurpose Internet Mail Extension) and PGP/MIME, a competing standard developed by Pretty Good Privacy.

There are three main approaches to encryption. Today, the first method is most common, but as technology evolves, the process will become more transparent to the end user.

Method 1 The sender encrypts the file using an encryption application, and then attaches the encrypted file to the E-mail message.

Method 2 The sender's E-mail software encrypts and compresses the entire message before it is sent.

Method 3 The E-mail gateway encrypts all outgoing messages as they leave the corporate network.

Before the recipient can unlock the message, they must have the decryption key. This can be sent to the recipient ahead of time by the sender. Alternately, both the sender and receiver can subscribe to an encryption service that manages a security infrastructure on behalf of the E-mail users, ensuring that they both automatically have the keys they need to communicate with each other.
This encryption service provider may be a private entity such as VeriSign Inc. (http://www.verisign.com) who, for a fee, issues digital IDs to support privacy and authentication. Or, the company that the sender and receiver work for may have set up their own security encryption using a product such as Entrust from Entrust Technologies (http://www.entrust.com).

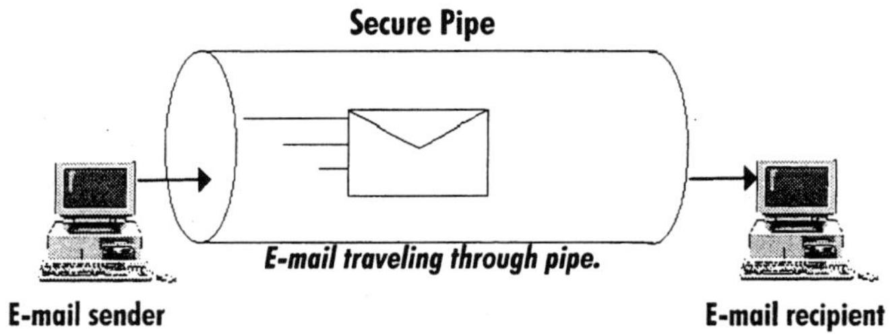

To find out more about E-mail security and where to get PGP encryption software visit http://www.well.com/user/abacard/pgp.html.

For Netscape users, Fortify for Netscape is an add-on product that provides security. Visit http://www.geocities.com/Eureka/Plaza/6333/ to find out more.

E-mail security gives you two capabilities.

1. Encryption seals the message so that it can't be read by others.
2. Authentication is used to verify the senders identity using a digital signature or authentication certificate.

Chapter 5-3

Frequently Asked Questions

How do I save a mail message?

If you are planning to send a message but you want to take time to review it first, you can save the message. Many E-mail clients will let you save unsent messages. If you try to close the message before sending, the software may prompt you to save it.

If your client does not have this feature, copy the text of the message and paste it in a text file on your hard disk. After you have reviewed the message and are ready to send it, recopy the text to a new mail message.

How do I create and send an electronic signature?

You will use one of these three options, depending on the type of E-mail application you have.

Option 1: If your E-mail client has an electronic signature editor, you can create your signature within your E-mail client. Some will even let you maintain multiple signatures to attach as appropriate to new messages or to your responses to messages.

Option 2: If your E-mail client supports attaching a file as your signature, you must first create the file containing the signature and then specify its location. Each time you send a message with a signature, this file will be attached to your message body.

BEWARE that your signature file must be text-only. That means you will create it using a simple text editor such as Windows Notepad. If you create the file using a word processor, you will attach unrecognizable characters and control codes to your message.

Option 3: If your E-mail application does not have any signature feature yet you want to use a signature, you must manually create one each time you send a message. Rather than re-typing the same words for every message, create a text file containing the signature. When you compose a new message, copy the signature text into the message.

How do I compress a file that I want to send?

It is a good idea to compress a large file before you send it as an attachment to your mail message. This will save space on your system, and is faster to send. You can compress each file individually using a file compression utility, or you can create a compression archive of one or more files if your file compression utility has arr archive feature. Once you have created the compressed file or archive, you then add it as an attachment to your E-mail message.

Imagine that your community has a can-recycling program. Rather than returning empty cans one by one, you decide to squash them and keep them in a box in your garage until the day the recycle truck comes to pick them up. The box in your garage is like the archive file. It can contain one or many compressed objects.

With most existing E-mail software, you have to compress a file before attaching it to your message. Soon, though, many E-mail programs will have a file-compression feature, thus simplifying the current two-step process.

How do I uncompress a file that I receive?

The hard way to uncompress a file is to first save the attachment to disk, then run uncompression software to extract the file. The easy way is to double-click the attachment in the E-mail message, at which point your previously installed WinZip utility will pop up and show you the contents of the compressed file.

Unfortunately, not all E-mail applications have a built-in zip utility.

To make opening a compressed file even easier, some utilities let the sender create an executable file that, when launched, will automatically uncompress the files it contains.

Compressed files usually have the extension:	.zip, or .EXE if they are self-extracting.
Macintosh files will have the extension:	.sit or .sea if they are self-extracting.

If you want to know more about the technical details of compression, including speed and performance figures, check out the Frequently Asked Questions (FAQ) found at http://www.cis.ohio-state.edu/hypertext/faq/usenet/compression-faq/top.html.

Here is a brief list of file compression utilities:

WinZip	PC	http://www.winzip.com
EasyZIP	PC	http://www.aksoft.com/
PKZIP	PC	http://www.pkware.com/
Stuffit	Macintosh	http://www.aladdinsys.com/expander/index.html

What can I do if my E-mail client doesn't have a spell checker?

Spell checkers can be dangerous because once you begin to rely on them you get sloppy. I have to be extra careful anytime I use an E-mail client without one. One method that works for me is to compose my message using a word processor that has a spell checker. I then copy the text and paste it into my E-mail message.

How do I re-use an E-mail message?

If you want to frequently send the same message to different people, save the message and re-use it. If the message is short, you may want to create an electronic signature containing the text. Then you can select this signature whenever you need it.

If it is a longer message, send it to yourself, and then forward it to the new recipient each time you want to send it. (Be sure to clean up the message text each time to make sure they know it is from you.)

Or, save the message as a file and then copy and paste the text whenever you need it.

How do I know if my E-mail client supports line-wrap?

Send a test-message to someone who uses an older Web browser for reading E-mail. If they complain that the text appears as one long line and they need to scroll to read the message, you know!

I am in the habit of hitting the enter key each time I get to the end of a line just to make sure that the recipient can read it. Your application may have an option to turn on line-wrap to make it easier for you to read messages that do not have line breaks, but test to make sure that what you see on the screen is what your recipient will see.

If your client has a "plain text" feature, turn this on to avoid malformatted text.

Look for these features when you shop for an E-mail client:

Wish List

- ⇒ filtering (including for spam)
- ⇒ search feature (to find stored messages by subject or content)
- ⇒ sorting (by date, sender or importance)
- ⇒ multiple-attachment support (and multiple encode/decode methods)
- ⇒ spell checker
- ⇒ auto forwarding /replying assistance
- ⇒ security/encryption
- ⇒ auto links (recognize hyperlinks)
- ⇒ ability to download headers only
- ⇒ support for folders/subfolders to file messages
- ⇒ password-protected in-box
- ⇒ integrates with electronic agenda-book/fax
- ⇒ auto page-break insertion
- ⇒ electronic signatures
- ⇒ multiple in-box support
- ⇒ distribution/mailing lists
- ⇒ connect to corporate and Internet mail

⇒ optional configuration for commenting on previous message
⇒ configurable for timed connection
⇒ mail-arrival notification
⇒ unread-message counter on each folder

Can I have E-mail without an Internet connection?

Recently, an associate of mine expressed concern about bringing an Internet connection into his home for fear of where his teenage children might venture. If this is a fear of yours, check out my reference page under home computing to find security solutions (http://www.ITcoach.com).

Another alternative is to sign up with Juno, the free Internet mail provider who you dial into directly. You can connect to their mail server by telephone without ever connecting to the Internet, yet you can use their service to send and receive Internet mail. Juno is free because it is supported by sponsors.

What if I move and want to keep my E-mail address?

If you register your own Internet domain name, and your service provider creates an E-mail account for you using your domain name, you can take your address with you when you change service providers. Another option is to set up an E-mail account with Bigfoot (www.bigfoot.com). Bigfoot allows you to set up a mail address and then forward it to any other mail provider. So, while you receive messages at "your_name@your_ISP.com" the E-mail address you publish is your address on Bigfoot.

If you have already moved, ask your old service provider to create a ".forward" file (dot forward) that will redirect all of your mail to your new service provider.

Do I continue to send my E-mail through my original server?

You could send through your server if you wish. Unlike with Juno, you don't need Bigfoot's software to send or receive.

You can configure Bigfoot to autoforward incoming mail to any service provider (ISP) that you wish, so when you move you keep receiving mail by forwarding to your new location.

What shows as my address on the E-mail?

If you use Netscape, Internet Explorer, or any number of Internet mail clients, you can configure your "reply to " address so that it points wherever you want.

Example:

Mail can come into Bigfoot and be forwarded to your local Internet mail account, and you can read it from there.

When sending or replying to mail you could set up your E-mail client to include your Bigfoot address. Everyone will know you by this Bigfoot address, although you are actually sending from an ISP.

When you move, you redirect Bigfoot to your new ISP mailbox.

Here is a list of some free E-mail suppliers:

http://www.bigfoot.com

http://www.valise.com

http://www.hotmail.com

http://www.usa.net

http://Prontomail www.commtouch.com

Part VI

Tips for the Traveler

Chapter 6-1

Preparing for Your Trip

"I have a bazillion E-mails. It feels weird not plugging in 15 times a day. I'm going crazy!"

- overheard recently in a hotel elevator

E-mail lets you bring your office with you when you travel. People don't need to know your location or telephone number in order to contact you or send you documents.

On a business trip to Virginia I booked into a suburban hotel. The next day I took a drive and found Virginia Beach. It was early spring, but the weather was unseasonably warm. The beach was almost deserted and every hotel on the strip had a discount room rate.

It didn't take long for me to pull up stakes and move to the beach for the remainder of my trip. I got a great view on a fantastic beach and even managed to save my client some money on lodging. The next day I got a message that a package had been sent to the other hotel. I panicked! I had neglected to tell anyone that I had moved! I raced back to the old hotel to find that, yes, a package did arrive for me, but they had returned it because I wasn't registered as a guest. That *never* happens to E-mail attachments.

It seems that these days, we are so dependent on E-mail that people just can't leave home without it. Whether you are a power-user who travels extensively, or the one-trip-a-year person who is just getting adjusted to how heavy laptops/notebooks really are (despite what the brochure said), there are E-mail perils to avoid while you are away from the home or office.

Just because you were able to access your E-mail with the portable PC you took on your last trip, don't think that it will always work that way. If you depend on accessing your E-mail from a remote location, here are some things to consider:

- Not all telephone connections use a standard service. Call waiting, tone/pulse cellular service, etc., can all affect your ability to connect reliably.
- Do you know how to adjust your modem settings to compensate for the telephone service?
- Do you have a backup plan if the telephone line is busy or out of service?
- Do people know how to reach you by means other than E-mail? What if there is a problem with your E-mail server or Internet Service Provider?
- Messages with large attachments can take an exceedingly long time to access. Are people who send mail to you aware of this?
- Consider how you use the "out-of-office reply" function since you are out of the office but still receiving and replying to your mail.
- Unless you have two separate telephone lines, you will not be able to contact technical support while you are trying to connect. This makes troubleshooting difficult.
- Know the limitations of your long-distance service.

You can do a few things *before* you leave on your trip to prevent problems collecting your E-mail while you are traveling:

Gather the necessary hardware

It never fails. The phone jack in the hotel is always hidden behind the bed. Be sure to pack a spare telephone extension cord as well as other items you may need, such as that little "dongle" that came with your portable computer's modem... *"Now where did I put that thing anyway?"* Some common items you will need are listed at the end of this chapter.

Buy two of everything

Don't rely on your memory to make sure that you have everything that you need. "*Honey, is there a little dangly thing on my desk where I usually keep my computer?*" Keep a separate laptop bag packed with all of the things you will need while on the road. If you need cables, etc. both at home and on the road, buy a second set to leave packed. Keep a list of what you need.

Keep all loose attachments in a zip-lock bag or pouch

WAYNE'S RULE OF PACKING

If there is a loose seam or fold in your luggage that tiny bits can get lost in, they will. And, you will only find them the day after you come home. Collect all of the loose items and cables in one spot. A zip-lock bag from the kitchen will work, but you can also buy small nylon bags to fit into your luggage.

Gather the local-access telephone numbers before you leave

If you will be calling a local telephone number to connect to the Internet or corporate mail while you are away, be sure to get the correct numbers before you leave. You may also want to get a list of alternate numbers in case there is a problem from your location.

Configure your system to connect, and test it before leaving

Before you leave for your trip, pre-configure your system to connect using the remote-access telephone number that you will use on the road. With many systems, you can create separate "profiles" for each location you will call. Although it will cost you some long-distance charges for those test calls, it is much cheaper than trying to call long distance for technical support if things go wrong.

Write a how-to-connect instruction guide

Don't re-invent the wheel each time you go on the road. The less frequently you travel the more likely it is that you will forget how you connected the last time. Invest some time now to write an instruction guide for yourself. Perhaps your company can create a connection guide to be used by others as well.

Gather technical support telephone phone numbers

Before you need it, find out where to call if you have problems connecting. If you *do* call for help, be pleasant at all cost! They say that the squeaky wheel gets the oil. If you are dangling precariously by a thin telephone line, the last thing you need is oil!

Learn to use alternate connect methods before you need them

There are many alternative methods of receiving mail remotely. On many of my trips, I don't even bring a laptop anymore. As long as I can find a computer with an Internet connection, I'm set. You can find out more about remote access alternatives, such as the Web, later in this section.

Remote E-mail Packing List

- Computer or palm-top computer
- Modem
- Power supply (does your modem also require its own?)
- Power cords
- Telephone cord (a long one or an extension)
- Splitter that allows you to connect your laptop and telephone to the same outlet
- Adapter to plug your modem into your telephone line (a "dongle")
- Modem cable (if you have an external modem)
- List of telephone numbers (technical support and local access)
- Remote-user manual (I can prepare one for your company. Drop me a line at info@ITcoach.com.)

Test everything before you leave.

Chapter 6-2

Setting up Your Office Before You Leave

"On the road again... just can't wait to get on the road again."

Willie Nelson

Do you really want to be burdened with E-mail on your next pleasure trip? Or perhaps your next business trip would be more successful without the distractions of the office following you. You *could* just leave without letting anyone know, but as a courtesy to those trying to contact you, why not at least hang up a "gone fishing" sign?

Activate the out-of-office reply feature

Some E-mail packages offer a feature to alert people who send you E-mail that you are not at that workstation to accept the E-mail. The system can be configured to automatically reply to the sender with a message of your choice. Some packages go one step further by allowing forwarding of the mail to an alternate address or to someone else who will be taking care of the mail in your absence. If you are using a corporate E-mail system, ask your system administrator about this feature.

WARNING: Be aware that system rules that are configured to automatically respond to mail come in two flavors.

1. **Rules are processed on your PC:**
   If your E-mail client provides a rules feature to automatically respond to your incoming messages, your computer must periodically connect to check mail. This means that either someone at your office must turn your computer on from time to time, or it must be left turned on and configured to automatically check for mail every few hours. Automatic connection should be a feature of your E-mail client. Eudora Mail, Microsoft Outlook 98 and a host of other E-mail clients provide this function.

OR

2. **Rules are processed on the server:**
   Microsoft Exchange, Novell's GroupWise, and Banyan's Beyond Mail are examples of corporate E-mail systems that allow the user to configure rules for the server to automatically route, sort, or respond to incoming messages. If the server knows what to do, your computer never needs to be turned on.

Use "Internet E-mail vacationing" to let correspondents know you're away

If you use Internet mail, your service provider can help you create a ".forward" (referred to as a "dot forward") file and place it on your server so that any incoming mail will be forwarded to an alternate address.

Your service provider may also have an easier way to notify users that you will be away. Magma Communications Ltd., for example, provides its users with a form to configure "E-mail vacationing" using their Internet browser.

***WARNING*:** If your E-mail system is set to reply to incoming messages, it will also reply to any mailing lists you belong to. Your reply might go out to hundreds of people.

Sample "E-mail vacationing" message:

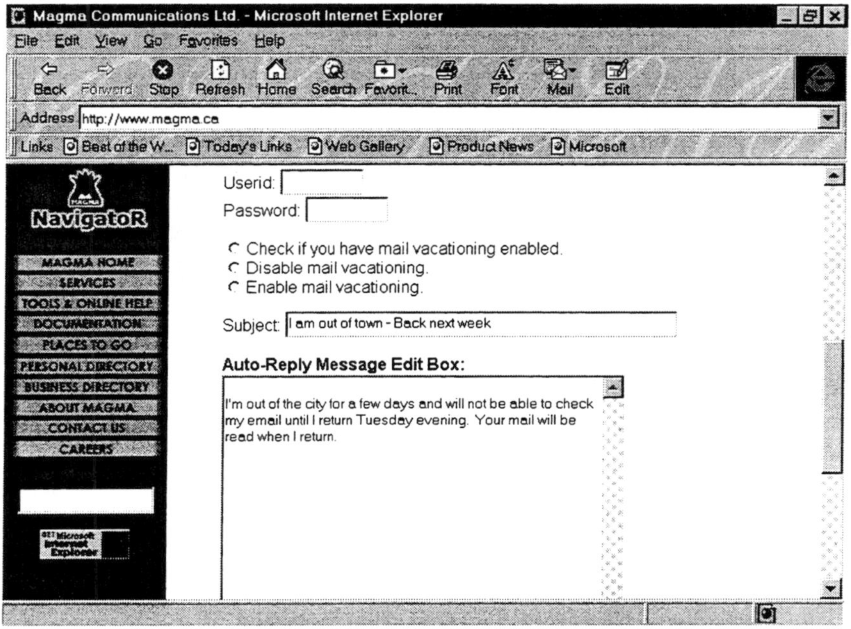

WARNING: If you set up a rule to deal with mail in your absence, be aware that you may cause difficulties if you check your mail while you are away. For example, if you send an automated reply indicating that you are absent, you will typically leave the message in your in-box. If you automatically forward it to someone else, are you keeping a copy for yourself?

Also, when your mail is read it is typically removed from the E-mail server. If your personal computer is configured to automatically check your mail, you may have to wait until you return to the office to read any new messages.

Avoid the continuous-forwarding loop

If you configure your E-mail system to automatically forward your messages to someone else, what happens if they are away and forward their mail to you? Check with your system administrator to find out how your system deals with this possibility.

Set up your voice mail

When you record your voice mail message indicating that you will be away, you may want to leave details on when you will return and where you can be reached. Let the caller know what your preferred communication method is and include your E-mail address.

Chapter 6-3

Reducing Remote Connection Costs

Short E-mail notes containing nothing but text are quick to download. Time spent reading E-mail messages off-line (when not connected) costs you only your time. But multiply the time to download one E-mail message by one hundred or more, and costs will quickly add up. Add to that the extra time it takes to download messages with attachments, and connect time escalates dramatically. The farther you are from home, the more expensive your messages are.

There are many ways to reduce the cost of accessing E-mail, but each method has its drawbacks.

Set up a 1-800 toll-free number

My friends say that I am a penny-pincher, a point that I do not dispute. It's not that I won't pay the price for something of value to me, it's just that I spend as little as possible on the necessities so that I will have more to spend on the pleasures in life. Fine dining may be one person's pleasure, but I would rather save my money so that I can go racing more often.

Long-distance telephone charges are something we all try to reduce, particularly from a hotel room where a hefty surcharge is added. To reduce the cost for me to call home, or to check my voice messages when I travel, I have set up a 1-800 number that provides me with a better long-distance rate regardless of where I call from. And this number costs me nothing except when I use it.

Set up a 1-800 number for your remote users who dial in for E-mail. It beats paying long-distance charges at the hotel rate, and creates fewer expense claims to process.

WARNING: Some hotels now charge a premium for 1-800 calls. Also be sure this line is secure from hackers.

Geography lesson: is Mexico part of North America?

What is the cost of accessing E-mail from a remote location? Here is a real-life example:

A Canadian federal government department was involved in extensive North American Free Trade Agreement (NAFTA) trilateral meetings with the representatives from the United States and Mexico. Several of the initial meetings took place in the U.S. This meant that all members of the Canadian delegation were equipped with laptops and given remote access capability to dial up and retrieve their E-mail. Users quickly got accustomed to the ease and practicality of remote mail. Preliminary scanning of long-distance charges revealed the need for a toll-free 1-800 number to eliminate long-distance charges from anywhere in North America.

Then the meetings shifted to Mexico. The delegates soon found that the 1-800 number was not valid there. Ever resourceful and keenly intent on gaining access to their burgeoning E-mail, the delegates dialed long distance. The connection worked, but one month later a bill to the tune of $2,500 arrived for the long-distance services for three individuals for four days of E-mail connectivity. It is difficult to assess the value of the E-mail that the delegates received, but it is safe to assume that some of those messages could have waited until the delegates returned to the office.

This story teaches us two things:

1. If you have a local dial-in service, no matter where people are they will probably use the local number if that is all that they have at their disposal.
2. Be aware that all 1-800 services are not created equal, and make sure that you know the limitations of your service.

Configure your E-mail server to call you

If you have users who frequently check their mail long distance from home or some other fixed location, set up network access with Dial-back. Dial-back is a feature that can save money and keep your messages secure.

The Dial-back feature is supported by many dial-up "routers." The router is installed on your network and allows full access to your corporate network through a modem port. This type of connection is referred to as "remote node" and is the same type of connection that you would have with the Internet. The telephone line becomes a dedicated network between you the caller and the router that connects to your network.

1. **Use Dial-back for security.** Since a remote node connection can allow a caller to access your network, you want to restrict who can call. Dial-back prompts the caller for a user name and password. Once the router knows who you are, it hangs up and calls you back at your pre-determined location. If you are not at that number, you don't get the call and don't get connected.
2. **Use Dial-back so the company pays for the call.** Many routers also support dial-back where the caller specifies the number they will be called at. This is *not* a security feature. Since the company calls the user, the company pays for long distance charges. This method will not work if the call must be routed through a switchboard, since the receptionist will not know that the modem squeal coming through the receiver needs to be re-directed to a particular extension.
3. **Automatically reroute messages using Continuous Dial-back.** If you have a remote office where people will need to call from, have your router configured to continuously call the remote number. When someone needs to connect to you, they plug their modem into this line and answer it. Just be sure that there isn't a telephone plugged into it, or it will drive you nuts.☺

Avoid calling from the hotel

Hotels increase their revenues by applying a surcharge to any outgoing long-distance calls. Calling cards can be used to avoid the higher long-distance charges, but many hotels also charge for toll free calls that exceed a certain duration.

Instead of just charging a premium without adding value, many now offer high-speed Internet connections in their guest rooms. To find out more visit ATCOM (http://www.atcominfo.com).

Use someone else's network

Rather than calling long distance from a far-off location, why not find a local telephone number that can be used to plug into someone else's network? Many Internet Service Providers have established affiliations with their counterparts in other cities. Through reciprocal agreements you can call the local service provider's number, and ride the Internet to your home office.

Be aware that to prevent spammers from using your service provider's E-mail server for sending mail, you may not be allowed to send outgoing mail unless you are connected directly to your ISP or one of its affiliates. Ask your service provider to allow connections from an alternate provider.

Many corporate networks have attachments to the Internet so that users can access their mailbox using a local service provider.

When I travel, I use my CompuServe account to connect to the Internet. From there I can check my Internet E-mail. I maintain a CompuServe account specifically for this because they have nodes all over the world. Alternatively, you could just use CompuServe's E-mail service if it provides you with the necessary features.

Other networks you might use include:

- An affiliate of your Internet Service Provider (ISP)
- CompuServe/AOL (America Online)
- A closer node on your corporate network if it spans the country
- Internet cafés or airport terminals.

Work off-line

Most E-mail applications (Internet or proprietary) provide some form of working off-line. Messages can be composed before connecting, and then sent once a connection is established. Most Internet users are used to this, and it may also be available on your corporate E-mail application. Once connected, you can download new messages and then quickly disconnect to save charges. Now that you have your new E-mail messages you can read them off-line at your leisure, and respond as necessary. Any responses will sit in your out-box until the next time you connect.

Compress attachments

If you were to ship this book as a gift to a friend in a far-off location, would you pack it in a 10-foot by 10-foot box filled with packing material? No, you would slip it into a small bubble-pack envelope at a fraction of the size and cost.

When you E-mail an attachment, you probably over-pack. Why not place your message in the smallest container possible? If the message was written on the outside of a balloon, it would have more impact when the balloon was inflated, but you would probably let all of the air out first, ship it and then have the recipient re-inflate it.

Most pictures and documents that you send can be deflated or compressed considerably. Using a file-compression utility you can remove all of the fluff and packing and compress the item to a fraction of its original size.

There are several reasons to zip up the files that you send. Compression:

- saves time
- saves space
- requires less bandwidth
- is more secure.

Documents contain far more empty space than they contain actual text. Why send the empty spaces? Pictures with white backgrounds, or even black backgrounds for that matter, contain many repetitive patterns. Compression utilities make note of all of the repetitive patterns, and their location in the document, and then send just this information rather than the patterns themselves. As an example, count how many times the word pattern "ac" appears in this one paragraph. And how many spaces are there?

Download message headers only

Depending on the E-mail service you use, you may have the option of downloading just the headers instead of entire messages. For users who receive dozens of E-mail messages each day (including messages with attachments), this feature can save considerable connect time.

If you have the headers you can then sort through the awaiting messages and select which ones to download, leaving the remainder on the server until you return to the office. You may even decide to delete certain messages before reading them.

Chapter 6-4

Remote Access Alternatives

E-mail is just another computer program. It consists of an executable code that must be stored on a hard disk and then loaded into your computer's memory. Once there, your computer's Central Processing Unit (CPU) executes the instructions. The application is stored on your own hard disk, but the data can be stored either locally on your computer or on a mail server on your computer network. The network may very well be the Internet. If you are fortunate, you have a friend, neighbor or technical support person to call on if you have problems with your PC.

If you work for a large organization, you probably are connected to the company's own computer network, their intranet. Your computer uses this network to transfer your E-mail messages to and from the E-mail server.

If you work at home, or connect to the Internet to retrieve your mail, your telephone line becomes your network connection. This is known as a "remote node" connection since your computer is a node connected remotely to the network.

The problem with remote node connections is that the telephone line is not as fast as the computer network where the E-mail server resides, so transferring your messages can take a long time. There are faster communications methods than the telephone line. You may have an "Integrated Services Digital Network" (ISDN) connection, a higher-tech telephone line that transfers information digitally. Many service providers also offer Internet connections using the same cable system that your cable television uses. Regardless of which method they use, most people feel it is never fast enough.

For those of you who work at home or who travel, this chapter describes alternative methods for you to check your mail.

Fly by remote control

With a remote-node connection you must use the processing power of your computer to run the E-mail (or other) applications locally, and transfer the data across your remote connection.

Many companies use a solution know as "remote control" to allow users to dial in and borrow the processing power of another computer that is connected directly to the corporate network, just like dumb terminals in a mainframe environment.

The advantages of remote control are many:

- no need to install applications on your PC
- easier to support since the bulk of configuration is done on the corporate "server"
- faster for accessing large amounts of data remotely since the data does not need to be transferred.

Using a remote-control session away from the office, your screen displays the screen contents from the server you are remotely connected to. Your keystrokes are sent to the server where they are used to control your server session, and your PC is just a terminal used to control your session. Rather than downloading the contents of your in-box, you view the message remotely as if you were actually sitting in front of the server and using it as your own computer. The only traffic that the telephone line sees are screen updates and keystrokes.

Companies like this solution because it is easy to support. Any changes can be made at the server rather than at each computer connected to it.

Access your mail through the Web

Recently, a number of companies have come up with Internet mail readers that are available from a Web page. The page contains a form to prompt the user for their user name, password and mailbox. This information is used to connect to the user's mailbox, and the in-box content is displayed on another Web page. With cyber cafés and airport terminal Internet connections available, it is not hard to find a computer with a Web browser. Most Web mail clients will leave the messages on the server so that you can retrieve them once you return to your office. Some will let you download any attachment to the local PC you are using.

If you can find Internet-connected PCs to use on your travels, there is no need to lug around a heavy laptop computer just to read your mail. The downside is that you cannot easily take copies of your messages with you. Also, you can't file your messages and organize them as you can on your own PC (although this will change as newer Internet mail technologies allow you to maintain your entire mailbox on the server instead of on your own computer).

Work off-line

In the previous chapter I talked about downloading only the headers of messages, so that you can decide which messages are worth retrieving. Once the messages are copied to your local hard disk, you can read the messages without incurring any connect charges. You can also respond to the messages from anywhere, even if you can't connect to your Internet or corporate E-mail server.

Once connected, all of your outgoing mail will be delivered. It sure beats paying long-distance charges while you read or think about what to say.

Carry your office in a palm-top computer

You may complain about carrying a heavy seven-pound portable computer through airports, hotels and taxicabs just to check your E-mail. My first Toshiba portable computer weighed 20 pounds, so stop your whining!

But if you want to check your E-mail and must reduce the weight of your carry-on luggage, palm-top computers are a great alternative. They fit in a shirt pocket, weigh less than a pound, store your calendar and your contact list, and can provide you with fax and E-mail services through either a built-in or external modem.

These devices work in one of two ways:

1. Synchronize the contents of your in-box with your personal computer.

or

2. Connect directly to your E-mail server to retrieve new messages.

The 3-Com Palm Pilot electronic organizer is a great way to carry a copy of information that resides on your personal computer. Once you have used your computer to retrieve your E-mail, you can synchronize your Palm Pilot and copy the contents of your in-box. While you are away you can read new and existing messages as well as compose new messages and respond to others. When you return to your office you can synchronize with your personal computer, but you will still need to connect to your E-mail system using your computer to transmit and receive new messages.
Of course, you could set up a dial-in connection to your PC and synchronize your in-box remotely.

Other accessories exist for the Palm Pilot, or are built in to other brands of personal organizers, that let you connect directly to the Internet to send and receive new messages. Whether you are out of the office for only part of the day or if you travel on extended trips, either method can work for you.

Regardless of which method your palm-top computer uses, you are restricted to a small display screen. You will probably not be able to receive attachments, either.

Use someone else's computer

If you can find a computer with an Internet connection, you can probably check your E-mail. If you do not normally use Internet mail, your company can arrange for you to access their E-mail system remotely using the Internet.

A new Internet mail standard, called POP3, evolved a few years ago. POP stands for "Post Office Protocol," and POP3 E-mail clients can retrieve mail from any server they can gain a connection to. Chances are that if you are an Internet mail user you access your mail using a POP3 client. As long as you know your E-mail account, password and the name of your POP3 server, you can configure any Internet mail client to get your mail for you. Any personal computer with an Internet account has a Web browser that also doubles as a POP3 mail reader.

POP3 doesn't provide for sending messages, though. For that, you need to connect to a "Simple Mail Transfer Protocol" (SMTP) server (probably the same server that supports POP3).

Be sure to gather both your SMTP and your POP3 account information before leaving on a trip if you intend to check your mail using someone else's computer.

WARNING: If you use someone else's computer to check your mail, be sure to change the E-mail account setting back to theirs, or they will continue to receive your mail and send new messages from your account.

Netscape Navigator provides the ability to create multiple "user profiles" so that you can easily switch to a new profile to check your mail without re-configuring the original mailbox settings.

Many airport terminal Internet connections provide a POP3 mail reader. For a few dollars you can log in and check your mail. Due to the abuse spammers that have put E-mail service providers through, your ISP may block the sending of mail by anyone who is not connected directly to their network. If this is a problem for you, contact your service provider and ask them to add your alternate service provider to their list of allowable connections.

Technology is always changing and Internet mail is no different. "Internet Message Access Protocol" (IMAP4) is new standard similar to POP3, but more advanced. IMAP4 will bring many advanced server features to Internet mail servers. You can find out more in Part 5 of this book, "Technology Solutions to your E-mail Problems."

You can receive E-mail on your pager or cellular phone

Imagine that you are just leaving the house and you realize that you have forgotten the address of the customer you are to meet this morning. You call the office, but it will take them a few minutes to find the information, and you have to leave now. You hop in your car and begin driving to town. Then your office calls your cellular phone with the directions. You narrowly avoid a head-on collision as you prop the phone against your ear while rifling through the old fast food wrappers looking for something to write on.

Wouldn't it be easier if the directions just popped up on a display for you? Well, with digital cellular telephones and pagers, your office could have sent you an E-mail message with the directions and they would have been displayed on your handset. Many salespeople rely on this to receive silent messages when they are busy. Your telephone is given its own E-mail address, and you can also forward your regular Internet mail account to this address.

Forward your mail

If you frequently travel between two locations, particularly if you are using a corporate E-mail system, have your E-mail forwarded to a second account at your satellite office.

Keep in mind that additional E-mail causes extra traffic on your network. Forwarding every message can create a lot of unnecessary overhead, particularly if those messages contain attached documents. Consult with your network administrator to determine if it will be better to access your mailbox across the corporate network or to forward to your alternate location when you are away.

Would you prefer to have your E-mail messages read to you?

What is the future for personal communications? All of your messages will eventually arrive at the same place. Using your choice of access methods, you will be able to read or listen to all of your messages. The technology already exists! For both corporate and Internet E-mail users there are products that can read your mail to you over the telephone.

If you have a Microsoft Exchange E-mail server, you can use the Octel voice gateway, or if you are a Lotus Notes user, try "Phone Notes."

If you would like to call for your Internet mail, "E-now" provides just the tool you are looking for. Visit http://www.enow.com to hear your E-mail by telephone.

VII

Part VII

E-mail and the Law

Chapter 7-1

The Employee's Perspective

For many people, E-mail has become as common as the telephone. Unless you have been told otherwise, you probably assume that your E-mail conversations are private. Unfortunately, in many organizations your conversations may not be private. Company policy-makers may decide that all electronic communications are company property and can be observed at the company's discretion.

The biggest problem with E-mail monitoring is that company policy-makers and end-users approach the issue with different perspectives.

Each person has a self-determined moral and ethical standard with which they conduct themselves. Consequently, they judge their use of E-mail according to their own criteria. If someone comes from a background that says racially discriminating jokes are okay, then their conversations, electronic or otherwise, might reflect this. Those brought up with strict moral standards may believe that the use of some words is socially unacceptable and that anyone with a foul mouth will rot in hell.

Managers often create policies as a defense against the risk of someone's comments being attributed to the company. Therefore, E-mail polices tend to be rigid and conservative.

Is E-mail just another communication tool?

If you need to contact someone, how will you do it? Will you pick up the telephone, send a fax, meet in person, or send an E-mail message? Do you differentiate between the many methods? Does your company?

You probably recognize that the company fax machine is not private, and that it would be an inappropriate way to receive job offers because a fax message may pass through several hands before it reaches your desk. What about the other methods—they are private, aren't they?

With direct-dial telephones, we no longer need to deal with the inconvenience of unsecured party lines. And a private meeting is private unless it is held within earshot of someone else. My E-mail requires a user name and password so it must be private too... isn't it?

Is my E-mail system private and secure?

Don't be so sure. Here are some questions you should think about:

- Does your system administrator know your password?
- Do they have backdoor access to your data?
- What is your company's policy on snooping?
- Do they read your messages and track your conversations?

- What penalties exist for others who view your messages?
- Can someone intercept your messages?

The answers to all of these questions could be yes; in fact, assume it is yes until you find out otherwise. Check with your E-mail administrator, your superiors, or the human resources people in your organization.

In the *1998 KPMG Business Ethics Survey*, only 28 percent of respondents reported that their company had a formal program for checking the integrity of employees who had discretionary access to users' information. People with discretionary access include system administrators as well as managers.

My employer is ethical and would never spy on me, right?

As an employee, you may fully expect that your employer would behave in an ethical manner consistent with your beliefs. Sneaky underhanded tactics such as monitoring your every telephone conversation, the use of hidden video cameras in all areas of the building including the washrooms, or having a private detective record your movements outside the office, may not be consistent with your expectations. So, why would anyone expect that his or her E-mail conversations would be monitored?

Certainly, each environment is different. Security concerns may dictate that your employer observe your behavior in the workplace. In some diamond mines in Africa, employees are submitted to a body search at the end of each shift.

E-mail can be used to transmit huge amounts of data very quickly and easily. Your employer may have legitimate concerns about corporate secrets that necessitate the monitoring of E-mail communications. Each employee should be notified in writing if this is part of your company policy.

What is the harm in passing around a few jokes between friends?

If consenting friends receive jokes containing a level of humor that they appreciate, is this a problem? Is it any different than making a personal call on the company telephone? Have you ever sneaked in a few personal long-distance calls, paid for by the company?

The biggest difference, of course, is that your comments in an E-mail message can be attributed to you, even if someone else forwards them to the wrong person. An offensive E-mail message that originated from me and was forwarded to you by someone else incriminates me. It is much more damaging to me than someone standing up in front of a group and telling an offensive joke they heard from me, even if they begin by saying, "Here's a great joke I heard from Wayne; some of you might not like it but here goes...".

Although the original conversation started out as private, it could easily become public.

Here is an example to illustrate the point:

Recently a letter was sent to the Attorney General's office in the United Sates when a minority student in a Midwest college received an offensive joke. Actions were taken by members of the faculty to find and reprimand the culprit who sent the offensive joke.

This action began when a joke list was distributed with the explicit warning that some material might be offensive, and that if recipients objected to the list's contents they should unsubscribe themselves. Still, the recipient took offense and began legal action.

Lawyers can tell lawyer jokes, blondes can tell blonde jokes, and if you are from Newfoundland, you can tell Newfie jokes. Beware, though. In this case, the joke was sent and received by students of the same minority, yet this fact had no bearing.

Lessons learned:

⇒ The recipient may not know much about the sender, and so has no way of knowing if a joke is self-deprecating (poking fun at oneself).

⇒ A message might be forwarded to someone who will take offense at the content.

Will my E-mail message be read if I send it to another organization?

An excellent question—I'm glad you asked! While the risk that your message may be intercepted is one concern, quite another is whether the organization you are sending to has a policy that allows them to read all incoming and outgoing messages. As you can see, it is not just your own organization's policies that you need to be aware of.

Why does my company care what goes on in private conversation?

The argument can be made that the company is responsible for ensuring proper use of the system. If no action is taken to detect who is making prank telephone calls on the job, the company can be held liable for any undue suffering on the part of victims. E-mail is no different, but most employees don't see any harm being done as long as their potentially offensive material is not sent to someone who may be offended. And most employees don't realize that their comments can live on long after they have made them, and still be attributed to them.

When I delete my message is it gone forever?

If you verbally make rude comments, pass on gossip, or even let out company secrets, once the conversation is over it is over. If the conversation is in writing, you can delete any incriminating evidence and ensure that there is no written record anywhere. Unfortunately, if there is ever an issue of impropriety a message deleted from your E-mail system could come back from backup tapes to haunt you. Many employees do not realize this.

Your E-mail messages are stored on a server on your corporate network before they are delivered. If the system is backed up before the message has been retrieved, now there is a permanent copy on tape, which could be recovered.

What will happen if I break the rules?

Given that many employees may not realize the seriousness of their behavior, what response is appropriate? A thorough policy will detail exactly what the course of action will be.

Prevention is the best remedy, and your employer should make efforts to ensure that each person is aware of what is and is not considered appropriate behavior. Once employees are aware, then heavy-handed actions may be acceptable. Don't rely on your employer to chart your destiny. Takes steps now to find out what the policy is on appropriate and inappropriate behavior.

The Bottom Line

Although there will always be unscrupulous deviants who break society's rules, most employees don't fit this description. The typical potential offender is just going about their business trying to get the job done. They may try to break the monotony with a little human interaction through E-mail.

Education goes farther than enforcement to ensure that employees use the system appropriately.

Chapter 7-2

The Company's Concerns

E-mail raises a number of issues that do not exist with other forms of communication. The moral dilemma many companies face is whether or not to take advantage of the advanced reporting and tracking features that E-mail systems provide.

Rarely has there been a communication method that is so easy to monitor. So easy, in fact, that many features are built right in that allow long-term storage of a conversation by someone other than the participants in that conversation.

Data can be gathered to not only find out what was said, but to whom and how often. So with all of this potential power, should a company use its capability to monitor its employees?

Are your employees aware that you have this power?

In a private conversation held face to face it is difficult to record the flow of information without resorting to James - Bond - style espionage. Because E-mail can be tracked, employee usage patterns can be followed. How do you feel about measuring productivity based on the type and frequency of communications that an employee engages in throughout the day?

It is possible for a system administrator to snoop on employees' personal and business communications by opening E-mail. Because E-mail messages can be backed up or archived by the system administrator, a permanent record can be kept. All of this is out of the control of the typical user.

If your policy allows for tracking and reading employee messages, have you made others aware of this? How do outside suppliers and friends feel about *their* messages being read by your security people?

Why spy?

There are many valid reasons why a company might choose to examine employees' E-mail messages. Is there a spy in your midst who is selling company secrets? Newbridge Networks Corp. used E-mail tracking as one way to identify an employee who was selling company secrets to a competitor. The Canadian Department of National Defense cooperated with authorities to track down a child pornography distributor who was using the organization's computer systems.

Other reasons include:

- cooperating with the authorities
- ensuring that sensitive information is not exposed to a threat
- measuring employees' performance
- controlling costs by controlling the size and number of messages that employees send.

E-mail is better than a pocket spy-camera

Using E-mail, huge amounts of data can be sent quickly and easily to another location. Information-warfare experts tell us that an entire country's well-being could be put in jeopardy by an enemy that possesses too much information about how the country's financial systems works or about a leader's decision-making abilities. The same holds true for companies.

The first rule of negotiation is to know as much about your opponent as possible in order to predict their behavior. By disrupting your competitor's flow of information, you could sabotage their ability to gather accurate data. At the same time, you could provide your opponent with inaccurate information about yourself.

Can employees delete E-mail legally?

In an effort to preserve historic documents, many United States Government documents are regarded as legal records that must be retained on file.

These may include:

- records documenting the formulation of basic policies
- records documenting important meetings
- records that could be used for auditing purposes
- records that protect the rights of government or individuals affected by government actions.

Check out the United States Environmental Protection Agency Web site for a sample of records management issues (http://www.epa.gov/nrmp).

Is your E-mail system used for mission-critical information?

Where E-mail security is concerned, some companies have put in place policies stating that mission-critical information should not be transmitted via E-mail. If there is a danger that irreparable damage could be done to the company if the information fell into the wrong hands, a more secure method must be used. Other organizations have implemented a more secure system that can encrypt messages in order to minimize this risk. Encryption can provide two levels of communication: unencrypted for general communications, and secure for sensitive information.

The system is company property; therefore, messages are company property

Conventional wisdom suggests that the system belongs to the company, and therefore the company owns any information the system contains.

How heavy-handed your policy will be depends on the sensitivity of the information it covers.

A system used for the exchange of mission-critical ideas may well be treated with a very strict user policy. Cases where company secrets could be let out intentionally or otherwise may be reason enough to monitor communications.

Controlling use may be necessary in a case where the company's E-mail infrastructure is strained by the volume of information it carries. Many companies are being forced by system limitations to discourage overuse of E-mail.

Is it legal for you to monitor your employees' conversations?

You should be concerned not only about local laws, but also about the laws in the other states, provinces, territories, or countries that you send messages to. Is your company legally allowed to read a message that was sent to one of your employees by someone in a different location? What about your regional offices? Does your policy respect their local laws?

Have you made your policy intentions public?

Does each and every employee know and understand your policy? Requiring each employee to physically sign a document stating that they understand your policy is one way to disclose your intentions. Including a clause in the employee handbook may not be very effective since many employees don't take the time to read the handbooks thoroughly. You might consider a one-hour information session to introduce some of the key points of Part 7 of this book, and also use that time to introduce your company policy on security, appropriate use of E-mail, and information flow within the company.

Does your E-mail policy contradict your general policy regarding employee privacy?

Be sure not to send mixed messages. You may unwittingly be undoing your efforts to gain employee respect and loyalty by contradicting the company culture you have worked so hard to nurture.

What is your policy on dealing with offenders?

Once people know their rights, do they know what action will be taken for their wrongs? What steps will you take and are your employees aware of this policy? What should other employees do if they know someone is breaking the rules? Finally, what should an employee do if they are asked to break the rules?

If your E-mail system administrator was asked by a superior to access someone's mailbox, should they? What is the appropriate action for the administrator to take if this is against company policy? Keep in mind that it will be the system administrator's fingerprints that are left behind.

In the *1998 KPMG Business Ethics Survey*, 36 percent of respondents reported having a formal system for reporting misconduct without fear of retribution, while 22 percent reported having no such program.

Chapter 7-3

The MIS Mission

Management Information Systems (MIS) is the name that computer departments in many organizations go by. Regardless of the name your corporate computer group uses, their prime concern is for the maintenance of corporate computer resources, and ensuring the infrastructure is in place to meet tomorrow's needs.

Year after year, the personal computer increases its load on organizations' hardware, software and professional resources. As message sending expands, the sheer volume that an E-mail system must carry saturates the computer networks in companies around the world. It is a constant struggle to ensure that the network and related computer systems have the capacity to move the mail.

The burden that the end user places on support staff can be overwhelming. Meanwhile, the users live with the frustration of systems that don't always work.

Everyone wishes that technical challenges cropped up less frequently. The cost of maintaining the average E-mail system must be reduced, or at least controlled. While the technical support staff wishes that the end users would read their manuals and use the system efficiently, the users expect the system to "just work" without concern for the complexities and challenges they have a hand in creating. Oh, how unreasonable people can be. ☺

The policy agenda of IT (Information Technology) is to meter the use of the system.

If the technologists drafted an E-mail policy, their prime concern would be that the system be always available and able to keep up with user demands. They might say:

- Thou shalt not clog up our E-mail system with junk mail.
- Compress attachments and do not send them to multiple users.
- Don't E-mail large pieces of information.
- Empty your in-box. Why do you keep all of this junk, anyway?
- Become an expert—read your manual.
- We have been asked to enforce the rules, so please don't break them.

Technical support consumes a lot of resources in most companies, and technology keeps changing, so your computer support group must constantly strive to stabilize the environment and contain costs.

Educate the user

The most overlooked step in introducing a new technology is the question of level and amount of user training required. Training should not be like drinking from a fire hose. Instead of arriving all in one gulp, basic training should be followed by ongoing updates and reminders, using a variety of teaching methods. Introduce the E-mail-use policies at the same time as showing people how to use the technology.

The end user does not often learn how to use product features without some help, yet the computer support group struggles to encourage users to learn on their own. "Common sense" is used to describe practices that are common knowledge. But common sense has to be learned by each person in his or her own way. And what is common sense in one culture may not be in another.

In the corporate world, the two cultures of computers and business often clash over many common sense issues. This book presents the many E-mail issues that are taken for granted by those in the know.

Poor user practices often result from lack of knowledge about the issues. And awareness of the issues is really what your company's Information Technology group hopes to accomplish in drafting their part of the E-mail-use policy.

To overcome some of the problems that end-users create (such as overloading the system by sending the same E-mail message to everyone in the company), policy writers sometimes take a heavy-handed approach to system management for the users' own good.

But the goal of the MIS team is to design rules so that the system is not abused and can continue to function with the resources available.

Techies are the custodians

Your organization has given its computer shop the responsibility of taking care of all aspects of the E-mail system. If you are fortunate, your team of support professionals is customer driven (you are the customer). Far too often, though, a computer group uses a heavy-handed approach, resulting in a policy that overlooks many issues. This gives users the impression that their employer doesn't trust them and presumes they are guilty until proven innocent.

Strict adherence to policies is the nature of the technical mind. Technology troubleshooting is a logical process, so the technical mind is trained to think logically. If there is a rule and the rule is broken, then it is logical that someone should be punished. It takes a different mind to consider how the offender might feel if they were unaware of or misunderstood the rule, or if it was an inappropriate rule in the first place.

The MIS agenda is but one important part of an E-mail policy.

Chapter 7-4

A Balanced Approach to E-mail Policies

Implementing the Policy

Many companies are just becoming aware of the need to establish an E-mail policy, and government departments are no different. When they realize that the organization can be held liable for the E-mail actions of its employees, they tend to panic and create a restrictive policy to protect the organization. The rationale is that although they assume their employees are all good citizens, you never really know.

Although you are at risk without a policy, you may be equally at risk if you establish a policy in haste. We have all heard stories of wrongful dismissal charges as a result of an employer missing a step in building a case against an individual. Wording of the dismissal policy may have been intended to provide a company with a legal means for getting rid of someone, but it can also be interpreted as a defense against dismissal.

An effective policy includes guidelines for use. One goal of the policy is to state what constitutes improper activities and what the consequences are. From a legal standpoint, policies can be an important tool in the event of a difficult situation such as betrayal by or dishonesty of an employee.

Guidelines are suggestions for use and can be used to clarify the intent of the policy. They should encourage proper use, but should also encourage productivity. Guidelines written in a negative tone can discourage users who may fear that anytime they use the E-mail system they are putting themselves at risk— someone is watching over their shoulder. The undesired effect, then, is that they choose not to use the system at all.

Creating policy without the balance of effective use guidelines sends the message to your user community that they are not to be trusted. At a time when many organizations are trying to encourage their employees to be more entrepreneurial, this dampens enthusiasm and causes discouragement: "If you can't trust me to do it my way and do it right, then I just won't do it at all."

From a technical standpoint, you want to encourage habits that minimize the load on the system. For example, encourage people to make use of a central storage location where users can go for information, rather than sending attachments to each individual.

Then there is the whole issue of ineffective communications and overuse resulting in information overload. Many individuals complain about the number of E-mail messages that they receive each day, particularly in large companies or government bureaucracies. If you're preparing a policy, treat overload as one component of your communication strategy. Address how the system can be used more effectively, and take the time to look at how information flows within your company.

Many companies host brown-bag sessions to help employees deal with change. The benefit is a happier and more productive work force. Use the same approach to introduce new technologies. An instructor-led classroom session is not your only option. Make E-mail usage and information overload a topic at your next retreat, company meeting, or lunch-time event. Discussing the soft skills as they apply to technology can be an effective way to raise awareness and encourage the acceptance of new technologies or policies.

Steps for Implementing Your Policy

- Involve all facets of the organization when creating the policy.
- Make sure the policy fits within your corporate communication strategy.
- Explain why a policy is necessary.
- Explain the circumstances where snooping will and will not occur.
- Provide suggested rules for good use of the policy.

Establishing a good policy

Consider the following topics when formulating your company's policy:

- What is your policy if a boss comes to an employee and asks them to provide the contents of an employee's E-mail account?
- Can LAN administrators gain access to the mailboxes of their superiors?
- Who is able to read corporate plans?
- If an employee is suspected of stealing trade secrets, will you be able to prove it? What action can you take?
- Can you dismiss an employee who has inappropriately accessed information of others?
- Do you allow jokes to be exchanged between consenting parties?
- What is your policy on pornography or discriminatory jokes on the E-mail system?
- What is your policy on personal use of E-mail? Is it like the telephone, or is it only for business use?
- Are you allowed to monitor an employee's E-mail communication?
- Can you admit E-mail as evidence of alleged impropriety, breach of security, harassment, or violation of the law?
- Will you be able to prove that your evidence has not been changed or tampered with?
- Does E-mail have the same legal weight as paper copy?
- Do employees ever unknowingly attribute their comments to someone else by changing a message they received and then forwarding it on?
- Do you have bilingual issues to deal with and does E-mail conform?
- What if an employee accidentally intercepts classified information?
- If classified information is forwarded to the wrong person and is used maliciously, who is responsible?

- Are people outside of your company aware that messages they send to your employees may be read by others?
- Is your policy regarding employee privacy legal? Is it still legal if the information has been sent out of province, territory, state, or country?

Additional Comments

- A policy is used to establish a legal baseline, but may be open to interpretation.
- Seek legal counsel to have your policy reviewed. A poorly drafted handbook can actually be used against the company to prove the claimant's case.
- Don't discourage the use of the E-mail system by appearing threatening.
- Encourage system use by pointing to other resources that can be used by the employee to understand the issues (a Web site with answers to Frequently Asked Questions, user guides etc.)
- Make E-mail usage and information overload a topic at your next retreat.

Appendix

Books

p. 50 Miller, Julie. *Business Writing that Counts! How to write quickly and clearly in three easy steps.* (Woodinville, Washington: Fitz Press, 1998)

p. 80 Davidson, Jeff. *Breathing Space: Living and Working at a Comfortable Pace in a Sped-Up Society.* (New York: Master Media, 1991)

Web sites

http://www.Itcoach.com	throughout book
http:/www.dejanews.com	p. 33, 101
http://www.pearlsw.com	34
http://www.DrJulieMiller.com	52
http://www.spco.com/store/products/activemail.html	59
http://www.cvideo.com	59
http://wizardsoftware.com	59
about E-mail directories *see*	62
http://www.internic.net	64
http://sapm.abuse.net/faq.html	92
http://www.falkenstein.com	100
http://www.smalloffice.com/	102
http://www.netmind.com	107
http://www.parsonstech.com/cstudio/CardShop/	108

Index

Closing Thoughts

Congratulations on completing Wayne McKinnon's Complete Guide to E-mail! I hope you have found it valuable and a useful reference. If your bookshelves are crowded, why not pass it on to a friend or colleague, or donate it to your local library. I hope you will remember the following key points of this book:

Technology doesn't eliminate people problems

I wrote this book to help you understand about E-mail systems and how to use them more effectively. Far too often, technology is acquired as a solution to a problem, when in fact the problem is not technical. The fantastic technologies now available to help us communicate better do not replace traditional communication skills.

Hone your writing skills

E-mail was conceived as a sort of electronic Post-it Note, yet today many organizations use E-mail in place of formal written communications. Practice writing concise notes, but if your message is brief, it must be absolutely clear and unambiguous. And you can learn techniques to E-mail politely, to keep the interpersonal touch so valuable in business communications.

A well-written E-mail policy must be balanced by "best practices"

It is up to you and your organization to establish guidelines that describe appropriate use of E-mail, and the penalties that will result from inappropriate use. It is equally worthwhile to train your employees to use E-mail effectively. Establish your own personal code of ethics.

Invest now to save time later

Take advantage of the newest automated tools to help you manage your workload. In my own informal study, 90% of the companies I visited failed to take advantage of the time saving features their E-mail system offers. Set up a system for yourself to manage your information. If you don't need to read every piece of incoming mail, get it out of your inbox as quickly as possible. Take advantage of folders and off-line storage options. Remember that floppy disks are a cheap and easy way to archive old project information.

If you would like more information on topics covered in this book, please visit my Web site (http://www.ITcoach.com) where I maintain an Information Technology resource center.

I hope that you enjoy and profit from the use of E-mail, and that you continue to learn about how to make the most of your time, tools and technology.

The ITcoach™ Products and Professional Services

Wayne McKinnon travels widely, helping organizations make the most of information technology.

Keynotes and In-House Seminars:

Technically speaking:
Making presentations for explaining technology; including, marketing your products and professional services.

Stop being a slave to E-mail:
Avoid in-box overload and calm the calamity of corporate communications.

Branding "You" electronically:
Use the Internet and collaborative tools to expand your business.

Technology Trends:
For business leaders who need to make technology decisions.

The personal computer: unsafe at any speed!
How technology can hurt your business and what you can do about it.

Booklets:

Call or visit our Web site for a list of booklets by Wayne McKinnon, such as:

⇒ ***101 Steps to Safe Computing.***

⇒ **Tips for the Tele-Commuter**

⇒ **Best practices for corporate communications**

(Booklets can be customized to suit your company's needs.)

Contact:

Wayne McKinnon

The Information Technology Coach™

http://www.ITcoach.com

Phone: (613) 762-4608 1-888-712-6224

Fax: (613) 825-4895 E-mail: Info@ITcoach.com

Coaching:

Executives:

Are you a busy executive responsible for making technology decisions?

Are you finding it difficult to keep up with technology?

Wayne McKinnon, The Information Technology Coach™, can provide confidential coaching to help you with your technology decisions.

Product managers and sales executives:

Are you a champion for new technology?

Do you often hear that your audiences don't get it?

Wayne McKinnon has been making convincing presentations about technology since 1986.

Recognized as that rare individual who can take a complex subject and make it easy to understand, Wayne can help you plan your white papers and presentations. Wayne is also available to speak on behalf of your company at trade shows.

Consulting:

E-mail systems:

Are you getting the most out of E-mail?

In Wayne McKinnon's own study, the majority of companies surveyed were using only the basic features of E-mail and neglecting the ones that can really save time.

If you are planning a new E-mail system, or want to use the one you have more effectively, The ITcoach™ can help your organization take advantage of important features.

E-mail policies:

Developing an effective E-mail policy is important to your business. Equally important is that your employees understand and use the E-mail "best practices."

Wayne can help you develop a user-friendly corporate E-mail policy.

Wayne McKinnon's Complete Guide to E-mail

Could someone you know benefit from Wayne McKinnon's Complete Guide to E-mail? It's the perfect gift for people who send YOU E-mail.

Please rush me _____ copies of Wayne McKinnon's Complete Guide to E-mail at the price of $16.00 US or $19.95 Cdn. *including shipping and handling.* *(Ontario Residents add 7% GST.)*

I have enclosed a cheque or money order made out to Ryshell Books in the amount of $_______ U.S. ❑ Cdn. ❑

Name: ______________________________

Company: ______________________________

Address: ______________________________

City: ______________________ State/Prov.: ______________

Country: ______________________ Zip/Postal Code: ______________

Phone: Business ______________________ Home: ______________

Fax: ______________________ E-mail: ______________________

We offer discounts on orders of ten or more books. Please write us for details or call 1-(888) 712-6224.

Ryshell Books

Suite 531, 900 Greenbank Road, Nepean, Ontario Canada K2J 4P6